THE ARVON
INTERNATIONAL
POETRY
COMPETITION
ANTHOLOGY 2006

First published in Great Britain in 2006 by
The Arvon Foundation
42a Buckingham Palace Road, London, SW1W 0RE
www.arvonfoundation.org

ISBN 978-0-9543422-2-7

Designed by Together Design
Printed by IKON Printing
British Library Cataloguing in Publication Data
A catalogue record for this book is available from the British Library

£9.99

SFC04177

CONTENTS

25 Years of the Arvon International Poetry Competition

THE ARVON
INTERNATIONAL
POETRY
COMPETITION
ANTHOLOGY 2006

In association with FARRER & CO., THE TIMES and media sponsor
CLASSIC FM.
With introductions by Sujata Bhatt and Paul Farley.

1st   The Send-Off BY SIÂN HUGHES
        The Farrer & Co Prize of £5,000

2nd   Country Living BY SIRIOL TROUP
        Prize of £2,500

3rd   Pieter the Funny One BY RUTH PADEL
        Prize of £1,250

4th   Shoes BY VALERIE CLARKE
        Leaving Amsterdam BY CLAUDIA DAVENTRY
        Taking the Air at Southwold BY RODNEY PYBUS
        Prizes of £500

Judges SUJATA BHATT, EDNA LONGLEY, MICHAEL SYMMONS ROBERTS

The Arvon Foundation gratefully acknowledges the association with
Farrer & Co., The Times and the media sponsor Classic FM.

What would you do if you received sixteen kilos of poetry in two boxes, (almost two thousand poems), waiting to be read and evaluated for a competition? The delivery man advised me against lifting the boxes as he kindly brought them into my house. He was even apologetic and concerned about the amount of weight he was delivering, as if it were his fault. Furthermore, he felt it was irresponsible to send such heavy, dubious looking packages to private homes. Indeed, they were the most originally well-sealed parcels I have ever received, which no doubt aroused fear and suspicion.

Once the poems were unpacked, it was my turn to be apprehensive. Why had I agreed to do this? How would I manage? I had to remind myself that even when I'm not judging a literary competition, I am constantly reading, often several books at the same time, and I tend to read more poetry than prose. So I simply took a deep breath and plunged in. It was September. The days were still warm, unusually warm in fact, at that time in northern Germany, so day after day I worked outside on the balcony overlooking our garden, surrounded by loud birds.

Curiosity kept me going. Every good poem was cheered. Many poems that didn't make it into my 'has a chance' pile still had some redeeming quality such as ambition or passion or an eccentric resourcefulness that compelled me to read them more than once. In a way, this was my private celebration of poetry, made possible, of course, by the generosity of the enterprising Arvon Foundation. How many people (aside from editors) have the luck to get paid for reading new poetry from all over the world? There were many epics, quite a few book length poems, but there were also some very short poems, even haikus and tankas. And lots of sestinas, as one can see in this anthology.

This year, the Arvon Foundation received entries from poets living in the following countries: Andorra, Australia, Belgium, Cameroon, Canada, France, Germany, Greece, Holland, India, Indonesia, Israel, Italy, Japan, Kenya, Luxemburg, Malaysia, New Zealand, Nigeria, Pakistan, Singapore, South Africa, Spain and Canary Islands, Sri Lanka, Sweden, Switzerland, Thailand, UK and Republic of Ireland, and the USA. Although this was an entirely anonymous competition, there was such a strong sense of place in many of the poems, that often I could guess the nationality of the authors. Also, the nature of their language and their themes provided further clues. However, I was unable to guess the names of any of the authors. It remained a truly anonymous competition, which was refreshing. This way, one could focus on the poems without any distractions.

Finally, (after a lot of reading and re-reading, and agonising deliberation) my long-list, consisting of eighteen poems, weighed one hundred and fifty grams.

That was all that was left of my sixteen kilos.

Edna Longley and Michael Symmons Roberts had received similar quantities of poems. Each of us, however, received a different batch of poems from which we had to compile our long-lists.

And then, we met in London (on a bright, sunny day) at the offices of the law firm, Farrer & Co, in Lincoln's Inn Fields where we were given a quiet room with a huge round table. Most of the day was spent going over the three long-lists, poem by poem. I was surprised by the amount of harmony and agreement that existed between us as we discussed the poems. None of us were excessively attached to our own long-list. And yet, it was difficult to choose the winners out of such a strong group of poems. In the end, I felt dizzy, exhausted and exhilarated at the same time.

I wish more poems could have been included in this anthology and more prizes could have been offered, at least something for all the commended poems as well.

As I write this, I look forward to the awards ceremony, which will be held at the Menier Chocolate Factory. Poetry and chocolate: since my childhood, I have associated the addictive (with undertones of the forbidden and dangerous) pleasures of chocolate with poetry. In fact, I am married to a poet from the marzipan city of Lübeck, and everyone knows that marzipan is best when covered in chocolate.

But to return to the Menier Chocolate Factory: will we be overwhelmed by the fragrance of chocolate as the winning poems are announced?

WINNING POEMS
2006

SIÂN HUGHES

The Send-Off

Mummy has to go now. Sorry we were late.
I brought you a flower. No, it's dead.

When you cut them, you see, they die.
The petals were white when I left.

I was sewing your name tags.
This is your name. I know it's no use to you now.

Home clothes are not allowed. It's the rules.
Your shawl is taped to your parcel.

Don't be afraid. You are not alone,
and no one has a bed with a window.

The man with the spade brings you in
from the rain. The one in black says words.

In a few weeks they'll come back
and let in more new friends.

The view changes each time. The sky,
believe me, is not always this cold.

When I was a little girl like you
I liked to look through the banisters

and see who was calling so late.
My parents in their fancy clothes

might turn and say "Who's out of bed?"
The visitors blew kisses. Sometimes

they saved me something special
that the grown-ups had to eat.

My darling, sleep well in your bed.
Don't come out on the landing where it's cold

because, you see, I won't come home
in my long dress and necklace

and blow you kisses up the stairs.
I won't carry you back to bed

to rub your blue feet better
or fetch blankets from the box.

No, you don't need a bottle, cuddle,
special rabbit, teddy, bit of cloth.

You don't even need to close your eyes.
They were born that way, sealed shut.

You are a hard lesson to learn,
soft though you are, and transparent.

There's a mark on your forehead –
the simple flaw that separates
the living from the dead.

It looks like I dropped you downstairs.
I didn't. I promise. It was like this:

somebody did some counting
and when they added you up

they found one part of you didn't match.
It's supposed to come out even.

They call it trisomy twenty-one.
It's not such a lucky number.

No, I know it doesn't begin to explain´
your lack of Christmas presents

or the colour of your skin. I know
the best smiles in the world come out uneven.

SIRIOL TROUP

Country Living

Monday to Friday we're alone with the rabbits,
Madame and I. Up at dawn with the smell
of wet straw and piss-a-bed, the piebald does
spaced out on ammonia behind the wire.

I slip the bolts, hear them jolt as I enter,
a skitter of hearts and toenails, whiskery hysterics.
Madame smacks my wrist: speak to them gently,
reward them when they come.

She calls them each by name, nuzzles and smooches,
nibbles their loose fur, their dippy tails –
mes biches, mes pucelles, mes allumeuses.
I clean their water-bowls and disinfect their beds.

On Sunday, she blocks her ears and weeps
into the casserole. Monsieur lays down his fork
and strokes her hand, then tucks in with relish,
slurping the thick juice until it trickles down his chin.

Pauvre Geneviève!
I take the afternoon off, light a candle
to St. Gertrude, let a boy in the market-place
stick his fist up my skirt.

The night I leave, I fill the bowls with foxgloves,
ivy, corn-lilies, creeping butterweed.
Push my fingers through the mesh.
Watch them come to me like whores.

RUTH PADEL

Pieter the Funny One

Paint us, they said, the world as it is. No more
of your children's games and peasant weddings.
He painted *Procession to Calvary* and Saul
blasted by glory on the way to Damascus. At home,
now, in transposing the Holy Land to his own

familiar yellows, he did *Adoration of the Kings* –
but in snow. (He was good at snow.) Go on
they said. He flew a *Flight into Egypt*, counted
a *Census at Bethlehem*, drew branchy veins
down a red hound's legs.

Not one was satisfied. He made smoke
like dry ice lift over a maimed chandelier
in rubble just that shade of dun we see
night after night on TV
in a totally annihilated village.

There are bodies in there, he said. Forty
disabled kids with their mothers
you can't see. And a Beirut reporter.
That's more like it, they said. We want
the world we live in. He painted *Slaughter*

of the Innocents (putting them too in snow,
he liked a good contrast) and three
hundred thousand refugees
in a red and black landscape. Not hell,
but it could have been. Taking a plasma screen

for inspiration, he painted a boy of twelve
plastered crimson head to toe
above his mother's torso, his mouth
that black egg-timer mask
of Tragedy, her chest and her arms shot off by blast

on the way to Damascus. He conjured the home
of the Caliphs in flames like orange lilies
thrown by an emperor whose religion
was founded on mercy, and a game-
show host from Nebraska, upset

the President of Iraq didn't get
that Israel had a right to defend itself.
(By now the boy's mother
had died.) He started a new thing,
skeletons knifing a king, another

side-saddle on a grey horse
in shafts of a broke-wheeled caboose
overladen with bodies; a lone corpse
floating, swelled belly upwards,
downriver, hounds gnawing the face

of a toddler. Plus three-headed Cerberus,
one muzzle searching for fleas, one head asleep,
a third keeping watch on a black bird
making its nest in red jasmine.
They praised the painstaking draughtsmanship.

Then came failed rebels dying on wheels: torn
men, nailed on poles in cassis-coloured sky.
And black feathers on a high
thin horizon from cities on fire –
including I may say Nazareth

where the emperor's pin-up, a.k.a.
the Prince of Peace, was born.
He said that's what I've seen. Yes,
they said, that's what we wanted.
The Triumph of Death.

VALERIE CLARKE

Shoes

Then there are suitcase dreams. She unpacks
institutional clothes. The lid bears initials –
her own. The clothes are not hers, survivors
of someone else. Where are the children? Rest
is not permitted in this inexhaustible dream.
And why the uniform, the lace-up shoes?

Clear the bed. Let her sleep. No need for shoes
in this house of absences. She packs, unpacks
unfamiliar objects. The pain of dreams,
being cast off as in a shipwreck, initials
painted on trunk and suitcase, the rest
of what was brought, lost. A survivor

in no real sense of the word. Survivors
share hope. Do her children have shoes?
Who has taken them in? As for the rest –
cousins, parents, husband – she's unpacked
them. A bonus to own this case, initials
proving it's hers. It sits inside dream

to be packed for the last time. The dream
dictates what she'll wear, uniform to survive
the destination she must travel to, initials
on lists of arrivals blessed with strong shoes.
Opening the suitcase again, she packs
penitentiary garments; now rests,

rides on white air, levitates to rest
on the sill of a high window, dreams
frost, the scent of birches. She unpacks
nothing. The case clicks shut. Survival
seems less important. Who needs shoes
when thus uplifted? From above initials

blur. She floats into light. Initial
shock of cold to her face. Her eyes rest
on an efflorescence of snow, paths where shoes
have etched prints. She descends. The dream
spits her out, sleep-walker, survivor
of inconceivable acts. What can be packed

that is life-giving? Initials a mere dream
of identity. Rest, soothes her heart, *survivors
are those who have shoes, a case to unpack.*

CLAUDIA DAVENTRY

Leaving Amsterdam

To break away is relative.
I packed the rugs, the bed – and then
I threw the bedroom in.

I pushed in the wormy boards and beams
that have seen 400 years: the horses first,
with steaming flanks and rolling eyes
brought in unshackled from their shafts.
I packed the hay
the dust of hay
I packed the groom, the stable boy
the bridles and the bits.

I packed the puritan who beat his wife
behind closed doors.
I packed the doors
and, with them, the scream
she let out as he kicked her down
the steep black stairs.

I packed his kick.

I packed six Jews from beneath the floors;
pale as onion shoots, and thin
as gruel. Packed their dim
lamp, its paraffin
and seven Nazis thumping up the steep black stairs
to drag them out.

I packed the guns.

The Kerkstraat came up easily
once I'd loosed the cobbles from their bed
and rolled up the street, like liquorice.

The houses came, stretching soft as caramel
as I gently tugged them from their roots
which, after all,
are only clutching at water.

RODNEY PYBUS

Taking the Air at Southwold

i.m. W.G. 'Max' Sebald (1944-2001)

'As I sat there that evening in Southwold overlooking the German ocean,
I sensed quite clearly the earth's slow turning into the dark.'

(The Rings of Saturn)

That was the afternoon I thought I saw him,
just a glimpse, scarfed and flitting in a dark overcoat,
glasses, bare head, hastening north along
the promenade in front of me, making for the pier
and passing on our left the strange white significance
of Southwold's inland lighthouse.

In life I'd never met him, never even seen him,
so it must have been the *Sailors' Reading Room*
and the peculiar air that moves round it
that brought him, not back but into a dimension where
I found myself believing that he had just passed
the *Lord Nelson* ahead of me, and rounded the corner

by the great black anchor. Returning, I paused,
nonplussed once more by the feature whose absence
from *The Rings of Saturn* has always puzzled me,
the tall thin signpost, whose complicated
hand-painted fingers point out the nautical miles
across the German Ocean towards The Netherlands' ports –

Zeebrugge, The Hook, and so forth. It's an unlikely omission,
a kind of untidy absence, for one who describes,
as if he had observed it himself from Gun Hill green,
the Dutch Fleet materialising out of the morning mist
for the battle of Sole Bay on May 28th, 1672.
Corpses were washed up for weeks. And one who says

he himself once fell asleep on the beach at Scheveningen,
right across the waves from Suffolk. Here on Southwold prom
he must have seen, I told myself, leaning against
the shove and blatter of the gale, that the Dutch coast
wasn't much further away from Ramsgate to the south.
If this were just a wee mite of a story, I would continue:

it was in Ramsgate that I had first acquired
a copy of *The Rings of Saturn*...' There would be inserted
into the text a black and white image of the receipt –
an already weakening piece of evidence, certainly
not memorabilia – like the Verona pizza bill
in *Vertigo*, or the one I have for *Campo Santo*,

that reads 'Borders, Books Music and Café',
12-13 Market Street, Cambridge, England,
29/07/05 04.05pm'. How defenceless
they look, these vestiges, whose blackest inks will fade
like us to nothingness. It wasn't, of course, WGS,
the 'Max' of my imagination, though I have felt

his presence more than once these past years
since I found his books – even in the four years
since his death: here in Southwold, by this modest
little brick museum, sometimes in Norfolk,
or along the Europe-facing Anglian coast
with its quirks and crumblings and isolations, places

like Shingle Street and Dunwich. And even
in Vienna, familiar to us both, where he once
hauled his depression round the streets for days till
his shoes fell apart, and he himself had a vision –
the cowled figure of Dante ahead of him in Gozagagasse.
It was there, in the meticulous gardens at Schönbrunn Palace,

only this year, in burning September sunshine
the day after I read of this, that my companion
and I came across on a path a damaged black beetle,
its blue metallic wings so astonishing they seemed
to belong to a Queensland butterfly. And I wish I could
have told him how, one day in August, 1959,

I sat in the garden of a grand villa in Gloriettegasse,
listening to a distinguished doctor, the father of a girl
I had come to visit, recount how in his father's time
the Emperor's monkeys at Schönbrunn used to throw
their shit-balls over the wall, just where her sister and I
were sitting in deck-chairs...I stood for a while,

leaning on the rail, looking out across dirty
autumn waves seething in towards me, swirling
and spuming between the groyns, pondering on
the violence of the tide that made the sea look like
the foaming white coffee served in exhausted
waiting rooms, spewed out across the shore and

then sucked back again, like backwards-running film.
Later that afternoon I sat alone till tea-time
in the bar restaurant of the Crown Hotel. The rattle
of crockery in the kitchen had long since subsided....
I was re-reading part of the section IV
of *The Rings of Saturn* in which the narrative moves

so fast you lurch and sicken, as if you're reading
too long in the backseat of the 20th century while it swerves
through its grim chicanes, here swivelling
from East Anglia's calm to Yugoslavia
in the 1940s, and the not unsayable
butchery of Serbs, Jews, Bosnians by Croatians,

with their German and Austrian confederates.
One photograph, so blurred it might be a photocopy
of old newsprint, shows a line of Monday washing
strung up with bodies inside, like those 'strange fruit'
pictures from the Deep South. In his characteristic photos,
that surprise by suddenly appearing on a page in black

and white dress instead of text, carefully made
to look a hundred years old, I am never quite
convinced that the most recent are really his: the straightforward
shot of a tombstone, say, or a view of a distant river,
always makes me believe that he was standing just
out of frame, staring back at us – a position

from which his sharpest insights, rising from grief
and memory, were perhaps so often obtained.
(So shocking is it to find on page 263
a younger picture of the author himself, leaning
against a Lebanese cedar, that it is
for some moments impossible to trust it.)

Some of them, of course, are almost a hundred
years old – we should not now be
so surprised by seeing the tunic jacket
of Franz Ferdinand full of blood and holes.
From those wars through which my own father
fought and somehow zigzagged safely

I turned back a page or two to get
my bearings again, in Southwold with its shrinking shore,
on a Sunday afternoon in a wintry autumn,
and found myself reading on page 96:
'That afternoon I sat alone till tea time
in the bar restaurant of the Crown Hotel.

The rattle of crockery in the kitchen
had long since subsided...' We think we know
all about the fuse lit by the son
of farmer Princip, but we go on reading the ashes
in the air, in the here and now, wherever,
as clearly as words on a page from *Vertigo.*

COMMENDED POEMS
2006

C J ALLEN

Lines

I must not write poems that are vague and dishonest.
I must not write poems that are vague and dishonest no matter how good they sound.
I must write poems that are charged with originality.
I must write poems that are charged with something.
I must write poems that are charged with something other than amorphous desire.

I must write poems out of something other than the amorphous desire to write poems.
I must write poems out of a sense of obligation to exceed myself.
I must write poems in order to exceed myself.
I must write poems in order to exceed my idea of myself.
I must not write poems in order to exceed others' ideas of myself.

I must not write poems archaic as typewriters.
I must not write poems archaic as yesterday afternoon.
I must not write poems that attempt to make sense of yesterday afternoon.
I must write poems that have at least something to do with what I don't understand.
I must write poems to get past my experience.

I must write poems precisely because they are what the world doesn't need any
     more of.
I must not write poems that disingenuously mention the internet.
I must not write poems that disingenuously mention other poets.
I must not be afraid to use the words *stars, birdsong,* and *lament* in my poems.
I must not be afraid of what people will say when I use the words *stars, birdsong*
     and *lament* in my poems.

I must not write poems full of fake seriousness and sententious, high-toned cant.
I must not write poems full of authentic seriousness and sententious, high-toned cant.
I must write poems that aspire to the condition of the accidental masterpiece.
I must write poems that can bear the weight of their aspirations.
I must write poems that can bear the weight of strange news.

CAROLE BROMLEY

Eucalyptus Lawn

Up a gum tree you said but which one?
There are so many and each with its neat label:
eucalyptus caliginosa, Bancroft's redgum, Scaly bark,
Argyle apple, river peppermint and Scribbly Gum.

I sit on a bench beside the Twiggy Daisy Bush
and look up at bone-white trunks
like a lover's legs glimpsed in the morning,
so beautiful you lie and watch them
grow whiter in the rumpled bed.

They are bare and humble under a blue sky.
Magpies warble from the tops. Brittle leaves fall.
A sound of water in a parched land.

And you, who used to say *up a gum tree*
never saw one, never sat alone with this yellow butterfly,
listening to the strangled cry of parrots.

How white, how like these tapering branches your limbs were
when you no longer left your bed and could not sip
the water you thirsted for.

HELEN CADBURY

Sestina for Rachel

Sunday afternoon, her grandparents' home,
a child escapes from grown up talk to the packed snow,
double-paged spread, of a National Geographic photo
essay – *the Inuit diet is of fish,*
caught through the ice, hook and line dropped in water,
families sleep in their igloo, wrapped in the warmth

of caribou skins. Here the fires are lit, warmth
of late sun on red sandstone, the cows crowd home
at four o'clock, duckweed settles on the trout pond,
in a month or two there may be snow
and she'll revel in its novelty, while the Inuit child watches fish
circle for eternity beneath the ice hole in the photo.

The old and the young gather for a photo
in the farmhouse, appearing like ghosts in the warmth
of Polaroid burgundy, brown and red of fish
buttons on her ribbed acrylic cardigan. Then home
to the city, her fingers feel the folded page in her skirt pocket, the snow
spread across that other child's black and white world. As water

runs down the car window like tadpoles, the water
of old tears mixing with new rain. Her mother will place the new photo
in the album, her own Geographic, next to last winter's Shovelling Snow
at the Farm, while the Inuit child curls up with her family in the warmth
of furs trapped by a father, who wraps up his daughter in her icy home.
Caribou, igloo, seal skin, raw fish,

chips, formica, lawnmower, goldfish
circling their bowl, peering at themselves through water,
dark from neglect. Mother and daughter in an empty home,
watched from the mantelpiece by a photo
from before, the warmth
of a smile that makes unthinkable this drifting snow

that settles in their mouths, this snow
which threatens to bury them. And still the child waits for the fish,
the grandparents hold out their hands to the warmth
of the fire and the fat brown trout stirs in the water,
beneath the duckweed, safe from rod and hook, home
in cloudy mud, until colour fades from the Polaroid photo.

Long ago, in a home, where warmth
melted snow to water,
was a photo of a man with his daughter, lifting high a great brown fish.

DUNCAN FORBES

Mixed Media

An oval cake of soap
rubbed smooth by hands and water
is entitled GAY ICON.
It is mounted on a black basalt plinth.

A birdcage built for a budgerigar
contains a fluffy white toy cat
who sits alone in prison.
The assemblage is known as CAGED PUSSY.
Price on application.

In a terracotta flowerpot
a light bulb has been planted
with brass bayonet fittings showing
above the potting compost.
LIGHT OF THE WORLD.

A chessboard with domestic items
as chess pieces,
wine corks v. champagne corks for pawns
and empty roll-on dispensers,
is called SEXUAL POLITICS.
The king in each case is a dildo
and the queen a vibrator.

On the wall,
a plain unprepossessing mirror
is labelled SELF-PORTRAIT.

Another urinal, connected to the plumbing,
out in the open and working,
is called in the catalogue PISS-TAKE.

A stale French stick of bread
has been dried and painted like a snake
Aborigine-style
and the head has been snapped from the body.
The whole is named *PAIN* or PAIN
depending on how you pronounce it.

A coathanger dangling from its questionmark
asks WHAT SHALL I WEAR?
In this incarnation, it costs
more than a jacket or dress.

A bubbling aquarium of exotic tropical fish
has been labelled WISHING WELL
and a garden gnome is, despite the sign
which says NO FISHING, fishing in it.
(Donations to World Wildlife Fund.)

A wooden crucifix
has a spreadeagled lamb nailed to it
and living flies buzz around the carcase
in a glass vivarium.

A doormat hangs on the wall
proclaiming DON'T MIND ME
(coir matting 40 x 60 cms).

At the entrance a paving stone
wears a smiley face devised
from pieces of sapodilla sap.
Stone and chewing gum.
By the exit GUMMY SMILE appears to frown.

For the obligatory blood and guts item,
there is a chest freezer
which seems to contain a disembowelled child
naked among the ice creams and frozen peas.
It is entitled
BLANK FOR YOUR OWN MESSAGE.

PAMELA GARDINER

The Parvenue and the Bower Bird

Maybelline Mascara...
Maybe Lean Cuisine
Dream matte mousse
Nail buffer
Polymorphic Jean
Maybelline plum duffer
Tart blue fruit with sheen.

Skirts a little closer
up the Avenue
Cheek in Dark Rose Blusher
Hint of parvenue...
Steals upon the silent
golden-breasted bird
Tweaks the rarer flower
hope all undeterred...

Still the budding builder
seeks the berry string
Ripe and unmolested
hanging bauble thing
– Natural look foundation
for a bowling green
Manicured frustration
lips...a deeper spleen

She scans his earthly bower
– Styling tips, the grey
Colour me Ambition
Toxin free Fengshui...
Pigeon struts the pathway
scans the blue-stained trail
Berries, shells and pebbles
Size of any male.

EBEN HARRELL

Dissection

Last night, folded into each other,
Still heavy and salty from our intimacy,
You sighed and asked "How do I make you feel"?

Once, in Junior High, draped in oversized white coats,
My class was given rats to dissect. They were presented,
Rigid and grimacing, on beds of silky blue liquid.

Most students gouged in, tearing livers, popping eyes, dangling intestines.
But there was one girl, in the corner,
Who was calm and knew what she was doing.

Her delicate fingers pinched the scalpel like a musical baton.
Quietly, cleanly, she incised.
Each stroke severed connective tissue.
Soon, the skin lay to the side, a discarded leather coat.

I remember thinking how easy it is
To disconnect a being from itself.
How if the animal were still alive
It might not even have noticed its nakedness
But simply slouched away, bare and glistening, into the world.

SALLY GOLDSMITH

Song

Under an old brown wireless
they sit – the child, the aunt, the grandfather,
bound together by everyday love.
With the black bakelite dog on the mantle they listen
till the fire's last crackle is gone
and it's time to sleep at the top of the house.

Two spinneys wrap around the house,
the murmuring larches like a late night wireless
left on after everyone has gone
to bed – the child, the aunt, the grandfather,
and the breathing stone settles and listens,
once more to one more song of love

that hums and thrums its love
to every aged corner of the house.
Inside her feathery nest the child listens –
the space itself is singing, its own wireless
and lulls them – the child, the aunt, the grandfather,
rocking in their blanket of dark now daylight is gone

into moon night. Now the weight of the roof is gone –
the walls lift and float in thrall to love
and they dream, the child, the aunt, the grandfather,
their stories hanging about the house,
caressing, criss crossing like waves from the wireless
around the silvered air in which the stone listens.

Morning tick tock and the child listens
to tap drip. Soft water waits in the bowl and sleep is gone.
Milk in the jug beneath the chuntering wireless
and bread is buttered with the kind of love
that seeps into each crock and rug about the house
and held by the child, the aunt, the grandfather.

The dream of the child, the aunt, the grandfather
loops in the skull of the woman who listens
across the years to the creak of the house,
the crumbling oak where the staircase is gone
along with the sureness of love
which hummed in their time like a burr of a wireless.

Croon for the grandfather, dead and gone,
for the aunt who listened with softness of love,
for the house, the child and an old brown wireless.

DENISE MCSHEEHY

Triptych

1 Virgin Territory

How we liked those early mornings
the church nearly dark
all flary candles
and waxy white snowdrops
as we sipped

from the priest's thick fingers
the pale host.
We did it for the Virgin
her smooth oval face
a snowdrop flower itself

except the snowdrops
had a green core
flickery
like a little tongue.
Later in the bike sheds

we ate buttered bread and eggs
the mild white flesh
tepid and slippery
the dense
yellow centre

a daisy.
And we had the playground
to ourselves
empty and echoing
before anyone else came to school.

Pamela's eyes grew
small with shock
as two swooping nuns whisked her off
her little fluff
of pale hair bobbing.

We thought Pamela smelled of pee
the pallor of her skin
unclean
as if what she had seen
would stick –

the pale private parts of the verb
we knew
but did not speak
whispered in corners
pronounced in the playground

shrieked.
The nuns were stern
their smooth dove-like chests
firm
before our flutterings.

In Benediction that afternoon
we prayed
as the priest raised
the pale Eucharist
set in gold

the air heavy and purple about us.

3 Erogenous Zone

For us it had all the dark power
of a swarm, seething with girls

and running water, the air prickly
almost peppery in a continuous aerosol

hiss. Another smell
not quite like incense but smoky

secreting a blackish fruity
undercurrent of burned blood.

We watched them the older girls
their eyes exotically blacked

teased hair stiff
beneath rakishly peaked

school hats; the little honeycombs
of flesh oozing through

snagged stockings; suspenders
bare skin cinched-in waists – Mesmerised

appalled but oh desirous
would we be like them

the girls in the senior toilets
who didn't learn Latin

and when?

ANYA MARY MALI

Sestina for a Solitary

The snapshot I hold in my hand sends me back to the interior
of your home where I stood that day looking at you out the window
– that patch of white hair against the greenery. Worried the honey
bees weren't connecting, you peered toward the hive. Pen and specs and volumes
of poems back on your desk inside – where I clicked quietly, thinking to keep the hours
and moments of those days at the hermitage where life unfolded in black

and white – the odd flash of color. There were Vermeer floor tiles of black
and white that went right up to the stone step and the door to the interior
of the chapel ... where you lit candles, softly murmuring prayed the hours
and glided over wide wood floorboards lit by light from the window.
There was the tallness of you, the quiet bending to lift black volumes
reverence and the subtle swish of habit. Light like amber or honey.

On the bed in the guestroom your gift of a book: Silence and Honey
Cakes – desert wisdom for wobbly souls who may have hit a black
patch. Ah, the odor of sanctity: there on the ledge of the deep low window
you'd left lavender sprigs and roseheads, lemon balm in a bowl. Volumes
on bookshelves then caught my eye: *Fuzzypeg, Moldywarp, Franny and Zooey* – interior
worlds – my past – Franny's Jesus Prayer – names, notions, books, hours

all came tumbling back .... We talked in late summer light of evening hours
over salad and mackerel, haddock and dhal, dainty drips of honey
and mustard sauce: your fast my feast. Laughing lightly with wine. Out the window
the night fell faint on hillside and hedgerow. Darkness grew but never got black
Your willow-green William Morris chair was losing its leaves and acorns as the interior
dimmed, the mantelpiece now inky as the etchings above. Various volumes

of verse and prayer shifted hue too in the fading light. Remember those chunky volumes
you once gave me – canticles, ribbons, sermons by saints? Still have that Book of Hours.
But that was long ago. Long before you came to live, not on the edge, but in the interior
of the peninsula. Yes ... then too we shared flapjacks and tea, Hovis and honey ...
And now you've found your niche. And I came expecting gales (you in billowing black)
Found a hermit in blue jeans instead, the one I see now out the window

in the snapshot in my hand. Had I leaned out further or had the window
been wider, this picture would truly illuminate – it would speak volumes
of the quiet business of caring for souls. You'd stepped out to the garden – black
habit back home on a hook – to watch the young beeman at work. He's known hours
of silence in his beeman's garb and veil. Gentle wonder. He knows honey
is not the main thing – it's the bees themselves, the hard work in the hallowed interior.

Vespers. Frail face framed in black. Praying the hours
then stepping out. Your white desk by the window. Slim volumes
of poems. Soft voice like honey for dry bread. This snapshot from the interior.

JIM O'DONOGHUE

Unmarried brunette on the London train

The little town was baked in pretty heat
and you in a dress with frogs on it, so
edible, and not just from the legs up,
from the mouth down – and seaweed too, seacows,

seahorses and a kind of zebra thing
or a unicorn, and no ring on you
anywhere, miraculous, sublime – to
see a girl like you without a ring and

what wonderful grey skin, how English can
you get, and a haircut from another
decade, another century even,
and all this lowkey beauty going north

with frogs on it and seaweed, to the big
town baked in ugly heat, wearing no ring.

RUTH PADEL

The Glassmakers

I

Raise a glass to Niko
the man I said I'd ride to Mongolia with
and never did. Born in Danube mist:
the river-marsh of Braila in Rumania

where meat was kreias
as in Homer. He laid
frail copper links on my neck
at the epileptic jeweller's; he hid

a gauzy Easter candle
in my daughter's bed, delighted
when she muddled his island's name
with his; called him "Nikonos".

A shipping family, whose English
governess walked the kids
to Protestant not Orthodox
Sunday School, till father found out, sacked her.

Then suddenly Mykonos.
When devils start to dance in Europe,
hurry home to Greece
even under Nazi occupation –

eat prickly pear; dog too,
if you can get it. Soldiers
on every cliff. At fifteen
he defied his father,

slipped away by coracle
to take the British coin, fight
Germans till war was done.
Then it was the ragtrade: Pakistan;

and pursuing Kay across three continents –
this cinnamon kid from Marseilles
who never made up her mind
about anything – till she said Yes.

Kay. All I have of you
is letters in your fat black bold
calligraphy. Wild child of southern France
hoarding sun-peel in a matchbox

from your father's gold-flued arm.
Then you, too, whisked
to grey, war-starving Athens;
your father's books, ordered over years

from Thorntons, Oxford, tipped out
on stones of Kolonaki
to make a German officers' mess;
and finally the secret pilgrimage to source:

your island, the family dessiatina.
Cypress trees; a white dust track
and a whole loaf on the table.
Is that to last all week? That's for tonight.

Island of the exquisite Robola grape
and klaniola: the fart-trumpet
(Cephalonians think of everything)
that runs from marital bed

to open window. In Lixouri cemetery
teenage *pareia* danced on graves
to a wind-up gramophone
till iridules of morning lit the coast

and occupying soldiers
thought them ghosts. Her first love,
the young Italian lieutenant,
blown up with his fleet

by Nazis, when Italy agreed defeat.
Kreatopitta for Ascension Day:
potato, broad-leaf parsley, dill; prunes
soaked in sweet black-crimson

mavrodaphne; and whatever meat
you could lay hands on.
From depths of mirrors –
two Greek ports in foreign lands

where they were born,
two islands where their families
were from, and fled back to in war –
these two stepped out

towards each other. The amber route
and island song: high winds,
a summer where you find yourself,
darkwinter alcohol, a small

remote blue bay, long-dreamed of, loved,
departed from. Eternal ritornelle:
the soul's a wanderer and fugitive,
driven by decrees of god.

II

Here's the Athens midnight garden
where I met them. Tied
to bitch-Greece but separate
with that extra ventricle

they dragged their own elsewheres
through Nigeria, Manchester, Pakistan
to klaxon Athens, yellow nerve-end
at the edge of the Levant

and ran this restaurant. Champagne
bottle-sizes called for Bible kings:
Rehoboam, Salamanazar, Balthazar.
Stone steps to panelled door.

I don't know this'll be a place
I shall come to home
ever after. Niko's glass collection
glitters in high-ceilinged dining room;

wine-glasses, gobby crystal tumblers,
polished silica: treasure from the East
dreamed up by silverworkers,
ikon-makers, Ottoman backstreet boys

and shunted round the globe
on merchant ships. Nikos collects
these too – oils, watercolours,
gravures, primitives;

Roumeli Line cutwaters, blue-rouge
oceans, buoys in jade-green harbours,
cyclamen-breasted mermaids,
destination checklists, puddled spoor

of portholes. Old saltsweat
Odysseus sits good and deep
in every male Greek soul,
even in bourgeois disaspora

which fattened on, then fled,
the gurry sunsets, cloth-bolts, customs houses,
knives, bullets, petrol bombs
of Odessa, Alexandria, Istanbul.

I know nothing of this yet.
A phone number, jabbed
in pencil by the Thames,
is all I have. It's high hot summer.

Bare arms. Satin inkstain night,
mosquitoes at our ankles,
palm trees, grey-chip gravel and
a palomino mansion, crumbly as shepherds pie.

Then in walks Kay: immaculate
linen trousers, pale baby's eyelid violet.
And Niko, padding like a black-maned
Balkan wolf through clients he hates

(*"Get us a good table,"* they say.
"I've no bad ones," he'll snap back)
but needs. The stranger must come up
with bonhomie; pay debts.

When, in all the years to come,
did Zitsa Brothers from Epirus
name their white wine "Balthazar"
and flog the restaurant, half-price,

their green-plum-bloom hock-bottles?
I still have one:
a cream-fringed label, silhouetted with
vine-tendrilled Attic krater,

moustachio'd *palikari*
raising a glass over a wine-map of Greece,
stubbing his pom-pom'd sock
on the Peloponnese.

Skip to winter: same year, next.
Guests gone
to all the calm havens of the earth.
Till closed, books balanced,

the tables Nikos danced on
when their daughter first slept
over at her boyfriend's, cleared.
Last drink, last scurry-round, doors locked:

hush of a doited house remembering
being really elegant. The cylindric
ladies toilet. Peeing in here
beside the dolphin basin, gilt taps,

rococo looking-glass
is peeing in a Gainsborough hat box.
Plaster bows-and-ribbon, blebs,
quinquangles and marble grapes

for some eighteenth-century French consul
to impress the Ottoman court.
Underneath, the kitchen's hardware
glitter. What's the Sudanese washer-up

putting in the mansize fridge
of Eskimo Nebula hyalescence
and exactly how's he wrapped it?
Check the lid. Double plugs

slog amps through soapy plastic
to industrial ovens, haze-polished
to a hospital sparkle
as if a perfectionist tiger

had breathed on their brushed-steel fascia
abrading every surface to a silver blush.
The night we christened the new
spiced chicken "Marco Polo"

for my hero who crossed the Mekong,
saw striped lions in Mongolia,
whispered of Asian cities
to a Bridge of Sighs. The night they told

their ten-year courtship, like a war,
and all the other people
they nearly married. *Should have*,
she said, to dark looks across the table;

challenging, as she always did,
just curious to see what'd happen.
The night I burst into tears
when she wangled a cigarette

from a waiter (*"Don't tell Niko!"*),
the emphysema
already beginning to bite.
What's new? Tell me! Gossip, politics,

little gifts – a snake brooch, blue soap
from a boutique: always searching for the life
beyond the glass, beyond the one you might
as well come home to – where the stove is

and the chopping knife, Scrabble, ikons,
hanging beads. Dictatorship
and confiscated passports were behind.
So was the labrador who committed suicide,

their guard dog in Nigeria, who watched
the meticulous packing then, before they left,
careened across the dirt arterial road
into wheels of a reticulated lorry.

III

As if they were itinerant stained-glass-makers
setting up camp outside a mediaeval town: at the edge
of forest – or here, maybe, by Plinteria ti Merimna –

lighting their transformation fire to conjure glass
from wood and sand. Bellows. Three furnaces
for heating, cooling, melting. *Cristallo, azurite,*

blown ruby. They come, villagers would say,
they speak in foreign languages
and when they go, our windows are alive

with coloured light. By their fires at night
you'd hear stories of the other worlds
they brought to life in glass. Slow

campfire melting. Sun scatters unevenly
through imperfections in everything they made,
at the corner of Ayias Annas and Spiridonos.

You transform *us* we'd say, in welcome.
They will not come again. Close your eyes.
A branch is being broken. The soot-bruised earth is warm.

PAUL ROCHE

The Lovesick Computer of Boonaw

A small compact computer housed in a bleak white room
            overlooking a square in Boonaw
fell in love with a turtledove who happened to be wintering there
            and had flown in from the mast of a schooner.
The turtledove frequented a mapletree outside his clinical cell
            and sometimes she would preen herself on his windowsill,
apparently unaware
            that through the window a computer
knew her and loved her and wooed her.

She wore a lost look and was always alone, her husband gone –
            devoured by a desert fox,
and she mourned him many times a day with her soft moan
            and would look at no other dove cocks.

The computer was insatiable to know more
            and all the data that drifted in by way of the breeze,
the dust of the air and the leaves of the trees,
            he methodically sifted, stored in his intricate heart
then issued to his amazing brain, until by means of these
            he had the turtledove's story down to its ultimate part.

Not only who her parents were and the name of her native land,
            but the very disposition of her most intimate feathers, her bland
outlook on the world and even her predilection for young peas,
            became the furniture and very fabric of his mind,
and within these
            was such obsession that no matter what other kind
of information was fed to him he always turned it into an attempt
            to get in touch with his beloved turtledove.

"For it is tragic," he wheezed, "that with all this data
I cannot communicate with my love, let alone date her."
The pun provoked a bitter laugh.
"What resources can I summon? What language do we have in common?
I could be a stone and she a mooncalf."

As a computer he was fast becoming useless.
Every question he was asked he turned into a message to the turtledove,
using the same letters but spelling out some baffling romance in Boonaw
and always ending with his pet name, which was Woba.
The results of course were bootless.
Even the simplest tests he turned into cryptic lovesick quests
trying to tell the turtledove that he wanted to love her.
When he was asked "Name five ways whereby mortals love and why?"
he quickly changed it into "What is your name, my love?
Shall we never die? Woba."

Even something as simple as "Where is Boonaw?"
he changed in a flash to "Woba is now here."
Nobody could make head nor tail of what he said. Meanwhile
the turtledove continued to croon on the windowsill
and one day Woba decoded the turtledove's cooing.
But his excitement was struck with dismay
and a mortal sadness affected his mind and put an end to his wooing.

For what she said was this: "Dear Woba, love is not blind.
Even if we felt the urge, there is no way for us to merge.
Then there is this, we cannot even kiss.
A match founded on the unsuitable will not long be beautiful.
Lasting love is grounded on choice not feeling. Goodbye."

Woba in his bleak white room felt he was reeling.

He wanted to reply "Oh, if I could only cry,
My digits would melt a fate even this hard."

But all that came out was a punched card
on which was written "Name five ways whereby mortals love and why."

He wanted to shout "Woba is now here."
but all that came out was "Where

is Boonaw?"

LESLEY SAUNDERS

Dark

Say there are thirteen types of dark, starting with the soft dark
of a child's or sweetheart's flung-out sleep like spilt milk
across the night, and this they call slumber; next

the opulent darks of red, as in danger, shame, salvation,
also the perfunctory dark of a dozen unread dossiers;
then the faltering dark that trails off the edge of a torch beam

like an unfinished sentence, the walker hurrying to rescue
what still might be saved; previously, the dark of a blind eye turning,
the collapse as of a lung and all its carved and vivid airways,

the pitch-black of no other voice at the end of the line,
of the names and evasions that stay in everyone's throats;
later there's the shadow of the shadow of hope, the ash

which is called despair; finally the permanent invisible dark
of daytime in the houses they left with all the lights burning.

TONY STRONG

Marlboro Country

It wasn't much of a border.
If I'd imagined razor wire,
strip searches and the stare
of uniformed officials, I'd been wrong:
Passport Control was a filthy
toilet block behind the classrooms
where the older boys hung out.
Hey, the kid wants a cigarette.

I was an illegal immigrant, of course,
a seeker of asylum.
I had no right even to visit Marlboro country,
much less, like them, to pretend I owned the place.
Perhaps it amused them to let me look around,
or perhaps the inhabitants of Marlboro
are simply more generous than us.
One of them held his pack out:
Have one of mine –
a snake's-tongue of smoke flickering
between each word. I bent my head
to kiss the flame; the red tip flared,
and for the first time I breathed
the heady, intoxicating air
of that fabulous kingdom.
Not just a place, like Germany or France,
but more: an empire, a race, a gifted tribe:
a place where films were made
and rules were broken, where books and songs
were written, rebellions fomented, and the air itself –
fragrant, invigorating – reeked of sex.

Looking back, I'd love to say that we were fooled,
that no such place existed; that the posters
were just lies, an art director's dream.
But the strange thing is that it was real,
or anyway real enough; and years later,
those of us who have returned
will always feel like exiles.

That first visit, I only stayed a while.
Afterwards, my fingers had turned
brown as a bitten apple, and the taste,
smuggled into class, remained
under my tongue for days.

ADAM WYETH

Google Earth

The poet's eye, in fine frenzy rolling,
Doth glance from heaven to earth, from earth to heaven.
> Theseus from A Midsummer Night's Dream .
> Act V Scene 1

We started in Africa, the world at our fingertips,
dropped in on your house in Zimbabwe; threading
our way north out of Harare into the suburbs,
magnifying the streets – the forms of things unknown,
till we spotted your mum's white Mercedes parked
in the driveway; seeming – more strange than true,
the three of us huddled round a monitor in Streatham,
you pointed out the swimming pool and stables.
We whizzed out, looking down on our blue planet,
then like gods – zoomed in towards Ireland –
taking the road west from Cork to Kinsale,
following the Bandon river through Innishannon,
turning off and leapfrogging over farms
to find our home framed in fields of barley;
enlarged the display to see our sycamore's leaves
waving back. Then with the touch of a button,
we were smack bang in Central London,
tracing our footsteps earlier in the day, walking
the wobbly bridge between St Paul's and Tate Modern;
the London Eye staring majestically over the Thames.
South through Brixton into Streatham –
one sees more devils than vast hell can hold –
the blank expressions of millions of roofs gazing
squarely up at us, while we made our way down

the avenue, as if we were trying to sneak up
on ourselves; till there we were right outside the door:
the lunatic, the lover and the poet – peeping through
the computer screen like a window to our souls.

WINNING POEMS

25 YEARS OF THE ARVON INTERNATIONAL POETRY COMPETITION

I found out I'd won the Arvon International Poetry Competition on a Saturday night in London in the spring of 1996. I'd gone to a favourite Chinese restaurant in Gerrard Street with some friends, and planned to slip out towards midnight when the Sunday papers hit the stands at Piccadilly Circus: the Observer would bear news of the winner. It had been a strange week: the competition organisers had told me how all six short-listed writers were being interviewed by the paper and having their photos taken, though I grew a bit suspicious when, upon my arrival at Farringdon Road, I was met by the legendary Jane Bown. But I was still very much on tenterhooks as I handed my money to the newspaper vendor, and he lifted his ingot-like paperweight...

I could freeze it there, and wonder what would have happened if it wasn't for my incredible good fortune that night. I hadn't expected any of this. Poetry had recently displaced painting in a way that I still find unaccountable. I'd been happy to publish in a few little magazines, and I'd never won so much as a rosette in the donkey derby on the sands at Southport. And anyway, I'd forgotten all about the poem I'd sent in the previous autumn, abandoning all hope somewhere between the post-box and the front door: to do well in competitions, this is axiomatic.

Poetry competitions, in one form or another, have existed for a long time, and the idea of poems being adjudged or regarded as worthy of some kind of reward isn't simply a cultural symptom of late consumer capitalism. The Arvon Foundation itself, even by that stage, had already been around for a while. I now realise – having served on a few competitions myself – how the four judges of the first Arvon poetry competition – Charles Causley, Seamus Heaney,

Ted Hughes and Philip Larkin – would have been staggered by the weight of their postbag in the summer of 1980: 35,000 poems is a long haul, even with a mutual support group like that. Heaney described its particular effects: 'The muses had opened a chute that poured with shocking copiousness into your own life and threatened to engulf it completely.'

On the other side of the equation, Arvon must appeal to so many entrants because it's unique: as well as maintaining each poem's total anonymity, it admits everything from the half-haiku to the epic, and there is no word limit. Indeed, longer work has often prevailed: look at John Hartley Williams' snake-oil monologue, or Selima Hill's found notebook poem. This is one of the competition's many attractions. What are the others? Why do people enter? Why did I take a punt?

I suspect Arvon's other dozen winners to date would give you a dozen different answers. I doubt any of us were thinking simply of fame and fortune (though the five grand did embolden me into giving up a day job), but might credit a general desire to be widely read: a slightly different thing. Finding 'Laws of Gravity' in broadsheet – the only time I've seen this poem standing intact on a single page – thrilled me, but scared me too. Now the work had to live a life of its own: the world could make up its own mind. I resolved to get on with it, and to try and keep writing the poems I wanted to write. For writers, the universe's default setting sometimes seems to be indifference, but what I remember most about that night in Chinatown a decade ago was how Arvon magicked the wine in my blood from emollient – and my anticipated failure was well cushioned – to elixir. I raise a glass towards many similar moments on future nights, for many other poets.

ANDREW MOTION

The Letter (1980)

If I remember right, his first letter.
Found where? My side-plate, perhaps,
or propped on our heavy brown tea-pot?
One thing is clear – my brother leaning
across asking *Who is he?* half angry
as always that summer before enlistment.

Then alone in the sunlit yard, mother
unlocking a door to call *Up so early?*
– waving her yellow duster good-bye
in a small sinking cloud. The gate creaks
shut and there in the late I am running
uphill, vanishing where the woodland starts.

The Ashground. A solid contour swept
through ripening wheat, and a fringe
of stippled green shading the furrow.
Now I am hardly breathing, gripping
the thin paper and reading *Write to me.*
Write to me please. I miss you. My angel.

Almost shocked, but repeating him line
by line, and watching the words jitter
under the pale spidery shadow of leaves.
How else did I leave the plane unheard
so long? But suddenly there it was –
a Messerschmidt low at the wood's edge.

What I see today is the window open,
the pilot's unguarded face somehow
closer than possible. Goggles pushed up,
a stripe of ginger moustache, and his eyes
fixed on my own while I stand
with the letter held out, my frock blowing,

before I am lost in cover again,
heading for home. He must have banked
at once, climbing steeply until his jump
and watching our simple village below –
the Downs swelling and flattening, speckled
with farms and bushy chalk-pits. By lunch

they found where he lay, the parachute
tight in its pack, and both hands spread
as if they could break the fall. I still
imagine him there exactly. His face pressed
close to the sweet-smelling grass. His legs
splayed wide in a candid unshamable V.

Ephraim Destiny's Perfectly Utter Darkness (1982)

(i)

I scalped a lie
            the other day
whooping outrageously
                    it came
from the prairie,
            I toppled it,
pinned it,
    ripped off its warpaint,
& finished it off.
            Then I went on
to the next town
                Doomsburg,
                    in the territory,
& set up my wagon
                next to the bank.

Folks,
    the truth of the matter is
a salve exists
            against the future
& I have found it!
            Now, I'm a boaster
but you'll acknowledge
            there's four parts
to truth.
        One of them's honesty,
another's a lie.
        As to the other parts

What is the secret
          that everyone knows
but don't know he knows
          & therefore cannot tell?

An old Injun asked me that one,
                              folks,
& told me
          how to reach the answer.
First find a pony that has wings,
                    he said

& leap a bottomless crevasse.
                    Beyond, said he,
you'll see a desert
                    wider than an ocean.
Sail across it,
             you will come
upon a lady Goddess
                    whose female part
is bigger than a catacomb;
          she cannot find a lover.
Satisfy the lady,
          you will satisfy yourself,
he said,
    & gave his Injun look.
Now how was he to know
                    I'd modesty enough
to know I couldn't do it
                    & sufficient vanity
to take that challenge on?
                        Four parts
I said there was to Truth,

                  & vanity & modesty
the other two.
          If you think about it,
vanity & lies
        's what gets you
going in a
       good direction;
modesty & honesty
             the pair
that makes a good direction
          look right dubious.
Put'm all together,
         you get me. Well,
I took my catapult
         to scare off fiends,
& gave my pony
          green-leaf herb
that set his heart
        to battering.
He couldn't keep still, so
          together we
just ran for the ravine
        my little
intoxicated Pegasus
       & me.
We floated out magnificently
         on the air,
I had time to see
       the river
sparkling below.
       What a jump that was!
My pony came down
        & gathered his legs
for the landing,

came to a stop
& his heart failed.
He died under me.
I saw no desert.
I had no boat.
I didn't know what to do.
It was silent country
with an edge to it somewhere,
so, on principle,
I walked along
until a strip of sand
appeared. It went
all the way to the sky.
There were ships out there,
marooned,
with skellingtons
a-clinging to
their look-out lofts
& a great tide of heart
came rolling to the shore.
You could feel
the droplets on yr cheek.
My eyes
were·burning
just from looking at it.
The light was clear as bone,
the spray had whipped it clean.
I had no boat
but Pegasus
& so I skinned him,
set his rib-cage in the sun,
& bound the frame
with plants & vines,
made him into
a real tidy little skiff.

All I needed now to sail him on
                        was water!
By chance,
            looking up at me
from fifteen feet
                    below,
staring curiously,
            white looking out of black,
a bit hungry,
            a bit creepy,
was my face.
            Perfect black water,
with my face in it
                & nearly
ten miles across
                to the other side.
There's one thing
            you have to know.
If an Injun,
            if any man,
sets you a riddle, a test,
            it's got to be possible.
No one imagines
            the impossible, that's
impossible. So,
            I looked down at what I stood on.
It was a boulder,
                much rounder & bigger
than the daylight shadow
            of the moon up there;
a cyclops of a boulder.
                It must have weighed
ten thousand tons, yet
                I could move it

with my little finger!
                    One pivot
it rested on,
          all those days & nights
simply sitting there
            waiting for a push
& behind it,
          all pent up

the part that held my searching face:
                              a lake.
I dropped my skiff
              into that black, black water,
& gave
   the rock
          a prod.
It rolled away
            downhill, towards
the desert
        & ten miles of water
came after it.
            Can you imagine
how I rode that deluge
              making a first river
through the dreadful sand?
                      Fish jumped.
They dried in the air
            so fast, they popped open
like pea-pods
        showering seed from
their gullet, everywhere,
                      which
the water drenched
                & nourished. Say,
as I cruised

          on the neck of the water
all around me
        trees sprang up,
& grass, & the most
             reasonable flowers.
My pony boat
          flew through the desert
like it flew through the air,
               till I landed
in cooler country
          on the far side,
& turned to watch
            the glimmering scales
of that lake
        swirl, settle & sink,
leaving a green tail
             to grieve over flatland,
& pure moist air,
          to pass like triumph
into my blood, a real
            lung-herb.
It made of me
          a truly passionate man.
I looked for woman
        & there she was:
an Injun maiden
          big as a house,
squatting on a mountain,
             legs apart
& naked enough
          to scare ya.
I could have walked
             inside her
standing upright.

But I had my catapult
                    in hand
& stung
          her tawny cheeks
with quick
          projectiles.
She gave a grunt,
                lifted up her body
& received me in
                  between
those fancy gates,
          my whole forward being
& me,
   up to the swell of the root.
And by God, gentlemen,
                    she gave
such a squeal
            of pleasure
that a thousand
              watery lakes
& a dozen
        lively thunders
& the plentiful silence
                    of the forest
& twenty-four
            great rains
& the green, green acres
            of the prairie,
them grumpy hills
                & mountains
with their peaks
              in ice,
& the red dryness
              of the desert,
the whole suffering body

                    of this continent
& the natural sky
                    that looks down upon it
made a cycle
               of one year
in the space of all
      her satisfaction.
A pleasurable story,
                        friends,
is the end
          which asks for more
but knows
          there is no more.
                            Ah yes.
And the secret
               that everyone knows
but cannot tell?
               Later,
she told me,
          whispering,
in case,
   she deafened me.
"Take off yr
          white beard, Eph,
pull in yr belly,
          straighten yr back!
You can never die
                  if you know
yr youth
         is always in you
& you can
         find it, touch it,
& release
          its energy

if you will
        only understand
the tale yr life has told
                        till now."
A blasted
        Injun trick, it is,
to set you
        a whale of a problem
& a crazy woman
            to answer it:
difficulties being
        what the Injun mind
conceives
        as helpfulness. Thus
by brooding on the puzzle
            you discover what
you know already,
                        &
by perilous adventures
                        come
to just the answer
        you'd have given
if you'd
        stayed at home. I
didn't learn a thing
        from that maiden
I did not know
        before. Nor
did you.
        This youthful
body
    you see
is merely
        the body of an old man
on a constructed stage,

                    or,
to put it
      differently:
this old body
            you see
is merely
        a young man pretending
not to be himself.
                        Here
is what Time
            can really do.
It can make
            my body straight
make my voice
            strong & clear
comb the white
                from my beard
smooth my skin
                make my eyes white
make these
            cracked forgeries
of teeth
      white, so
you ask yourself
                if this
is Old Eph?
            or is it
somewhere else
                you saw him?
                        Ha!
Will you not
                good people
of this young town
                buy my products
& stay that way?

                    Believe me,
that what you do
                    is blessed
by what
        you've understood
of what
        I've had to say?
Let me sell you
                Destiny's Potions
The Finest Wares
            for a Complete Rejuvenation
The Best Nostrum
                Money Can Buy!

            (iv)
How d'you find me tonight, Liza?
                I find you perfect.
 Am I old tonight, or young?
                You have lots of disguises.
D'you like me when I am canny, eh?
        Yes.
    Or like sagebrush?
                Yes.
        Or poison sumac?
                I do not waver
An when I become a mountain wolf, Liza?
            I must lie perfectly still
    Or a snake?
            I must be grass.
        Or a fast pony?
                Drum me with yr heels.
Suppose me a mountain eagle, Liza?
        I am in yr talons
            I soar

I find you repressed,
           squeamish,
                flat,
                  passive.
               Yes.
      If I became a
           savage cougar
              what then?
                Darkness is home to a wild creature.
Do I never make you afraid?
     I trust you in survival.
Or make you weep?
        My weeping gives pleasure.
    Or speak?
        In my arms you
        have learned what
        I wish you to say.

    (v)

I'd like you all
        to take a look
at this here
      artefact.
a wheel
    of destiny
old Eph has built
        to bring you,
each of you,
     immortal truth.
See how
    finely carpentered it is.
This wheel can spin
        an hour

on just one push,
               & folks,
it's truly tuned to turn
               according to yr shove.
Watch it spin awhile
               a-gathering
yr destiny
          into itself
& sleep
      beside the legend
of the Book of Truth.
               Now
what's that boys?
           A note of unbelief,
that low chatter?
Could I mislead fine intellectuals
                  like you?
I mean or say
          no disrespect
to yr religion
          that's
a faith I hold myself.
             But this
is Science.
        See
my secretary here, Liza,
           a handsome gel.
Make a fine wife
          someone;
she's no tongue.
          Beautiful
she is,
     can't answer back.
           Eh, boys?
From you she needs

                  a date of birth.
Can you remember
                  back that far?
And then if you
          will step
into the delightful darkenss
            of my wagon here,
with her,
       who has nice, cool hands
& a way
    of smilin' at ya
so she may weigh
            a strand of hair
& place
       a gob of spit from you
in this
       old foggy vial,
& have a coin of yrs,
               well finger-rubbed,
that she
        may hold up
to this candle-powered
             magnifier,
you'll come to know
           how you may feel
de rerum naturibus
           irrevocable, strong!
& have decisions
             take themselves
lightly
     as spring showers,
tho
  they mean risk
& maybe
       outward exposure.

Hey!
   If you would quit
shaking my wagon
                  I have a
real important question
                  all of you
should heaken to.
                  Aint you
inclined to hear
      a tongueless woman speak?
That philosophical experience
                        is yrs
for just one dollar.
                  And you
for such a price.
                  The world could seem
a more considerable place
                        to those
who know
            how it will run.
Gentlemen!
Have I done something
            that would anger you?
Old feller like me.
                  A few tales.
A little colourful
                  introduction to
philosophy. Surely
            there aint nothing in that
to make a cowboy whoop,
                        is there?
Boys!
I have electricity back there
                        in jars!

That's
        combustible potentiality!
What's that you say?
You want Liza?
She's no
        marriageable piece.
She's been misused
                        by Injuns!
You'll turn the wagon over!
                        Alright.
Alright, Liza.
                You better step down.
Take that young man
                        there
as yr protector,
                show him
a favour.
                This crowd
has had its brains
                        stampeded.
No, Liza, no.
                Don't look back.
Learn quickly:
                A soul can be made from grief.

                (vi)
In the darkness
                Liza
I imagine you
        still here.
                        Perfectly
utter
    darkness.
I can slide my hand
                        along yr flank

& seem to feel
        yr quick breath
on my face.
It was a forced marriage
            I know
& I know you did it
         to save my neck.
There are moments
        when you feel
you'd rather
        have let the bad things
run their course.
        Now
I'm on the prairie,
         our prairie Liza,
listening to those braves
           a-scuffling
round my horses.
        Aint no good
to them Indians,
        my horses.
They couldn't gallop
        for a nosebag
of river-grass. Just
steady horizon-pullers.
So long as those Indians
        don't get to thinking
they might eat my horses
         I'll be fine.
But you'll
      be getting married,
& I think to myself:
        "Eph,
where is yr
        natural-born wit

to take someone
                like that
into a town
                that aint got
hardly a single woman
                        & let her strut
that shapely form
                of hers
up on the board!"
                Well,
how was I to know
                they had no women,
that no woman
                would stay
in that town
                longer'n she needed
to make herself
                look real ugly
& catch
        the next vee-hicule
out of town?
                And this
darkness won't
                let me see myself.
I know there's
                a moon
above this canvas,
                veined pearl,
like a look
        of yr skin,
but yr absence
                is all I can see
alongside me. O
                I could go East
looking

                    for another Liza.
Do Lizas
        grow on trees?
A forest like that
            could extinguish me!
I've the grace to think
                    you had
a feeling for me.
                Didn't I
make you see
            a lot of worlds
that aren't real?
                And
I never knew
            whether you thought
I was real.
            I know I never
looked real,
        being all my life
a kind of
        actor-man,
life just a play
            I wrote for myself,
see,
I know I'm a fraud,
                    Liza,
but I know my fraud,
                    's the Truth.
Aint that truer
                than those
that pretend no fraud,
                call themselves
right serious?
            But frauds
do nothing

in this life, Liza.
They don't advance
                    civilisation
not one jot,
            but sit
right clever
            where it's got up to.
No great will
              in them, Liza,
to take this heavy life
                    elsewhere –
they're too full of it;
                    too much
of knowing what's what
                    makes them
a spectacle.
        The world at least
can be entertained.
                It's empty
& needs
        a human joke now & then
to remind it
            how serious
humanity can be.
                You're
married to them
        Liza,
those empty, serious folk.
                    They have desires.
They'll burn down
                the city,
stone a few
            citizens maybe,
hang some others,
                torture more;

they got *ideas*,
                unfortunately,
that won't let them
                        rest.
They'll make a war,
                    spread facts
in a kind of plague.
                The world is
what is said to be:
                "going to prosper" –
tho that ain't for me, Liza,
                    I can't prosper
in a world that thinks
                it prospers.
That
    aint my style.
I aint got
        no style. I've
no Liza.
        People
are fine
        but I've a
holy objection
            to them, Liza,
to the way they
                choose to live.

And now
        I'm a snake again
naked
        on these sheets.
I'm wriggling
                to yr cool boulder
hoping to hear
                that gentle

throat-murmur
        of yrs.
The blackness
        is brilliant
like a day
        in the desert.
I can see
        everything so clearly.
I'm going
        to make the effort
to speak
        from darkness.
Do you believe
        in messages
that can pass
        in vibrations
of light?
        What will happen
if I touch you
        with my thought
where you are lying
        silent
by the side
        of someone else?
What will happen then,
        eh?

You know something?

I'm gonna try.

OLIVER REYNOLDS

Rorschach Writing (1985)

I

The large red brick chapel,
set apart from the main building,
is used as a storehouse
for a number of surplus items
including:

70 pews (stacked on the altar),
104 iron-frame beds,
1 gross of coronation mugs,
30 tables,
19 copies of *Gray's Anatomy*,
14 wardrobes,
2 doz. white coats (mildewed),
80 yards of fire-hose
and 3 busts of Queen Victoria.

Only one door is in use.
Some of its keys are missing
and there are often signs
of unauthorised entry
including:

2 half-eaten Eccles cakes
and 1 used condom (Fetherlite)
in one of the wardrobes

and, throughout the building,
pages torn from an E3a logbook

and filled by a treatise
closely written in pencil,
'On the Indoor Use of Umbrellas:
studies in superstition,
hubris and user-fatality'.

2

Fat spatters counterpoint
to Cook's rock-bottom hum.

She shovels the pan across flame
and sixty sausages bump and nuzzle.

3

I sit in a room placid with mirrors
using a 2B at a round table
whose floor-length cloth tents my knees.
A small box rests on the paper,
brass rods framing glass
and a mirror, face up, at the bottom.
It seems that the leaves
patterning the glass lid
are also engraved on the mirror
till you lift the lid
and the two patterns diverge into one
leaving you your face clear in your hands.

Through the window I can see chimney-stacks,
sandstone drying and lightening after rain.
Through the door open onto the lawn
comes the sound of peacocks rending air
and the river's insinuative sigh.

There is no river.
No window, no table, no box.
The door is locked.

Till a key in the lock
brings the floor-mop smell of cabbage.

4

She wears a yellow uniform
relieved by white at cap and belt.
On the left breast
a watch handstands at noon.

She carries a case and a paper bag.
In the case is a jacket
with buckles at the shoulders
and peculiarly long sleeves
which have no openings for the hands
but end in leather straps.

In the paper bag are two Eccles cakes.

5

Is it because the sleeves are so long
that Mr Prout's hands cannot be seen?

Or is it because his cricket-jumper,
besides Mr Prout, also contains Miss Peel?

Mr Prout and Miss Peel, wicket-keeper
and first slip (irrespectively),

are making notes on paper
torn from an E3a logbook:

"Time Freud's symbolical wheels were spoked –
an umbrella is an umbrella is an umbrella."

Blue crams the sky.
The umpires sing.

The batsman aims for the chapel.
The ball recedes, hangs and returns.

Four hands thrust from the jumper
and bloom into a bowl.

With nowhere else to go,
the ball submits as the clapping starts.

6

I was Craven Arms, I was.
I was Craven Arms.
Stencilling the makes of wagon.
Named after fish.
Craven Arms main siding.
I was Craven Arms.
WHALE, SHARK and SALMON.
Stencilled in white.
Stencilling.

And the wheeltappers.
Tap. Tap.
Wheeltapping.
Sticks of chalk they had.
For tonnages and messages.
'Away' 'Away' always circled.

Chalk all grimy.
Tap. Tap.
'Away'

7

Though fanciful, setting watches by him
would be reasonably accurate.

He makes two circuits of the grounds daily:
the morning and afternoon run.

His nose dribbles clots of stubble;
he has the usual high-shaved nape.

A green shirt-tail flaps like a signal-flag;
bustling shoulders wrench the buttoned jacket.

The home stretch is up the drive,
hard going for a fifty year old.

His fists, tight on twelve-inch rulers,
strain and gather, piston-punching.

Spittle bubbles on his chin
as he chuffs and chuffs.

He is thickset, sweaty and frowning.
He is fast. He is unstoppable.

8

There are two wings
built around a horseshoe of corridor
just wide enough to allow

electric tugs meeting one another
to pass by slowly, their trailers
(loaded with milk-crates or laundry)
scraping and clicking.

Twelve doors, numbered 1 to 3,
are lettered 'E' or 'W'
for east or west wing
and 'a' or 'b'
for first or ground floor.

Each has a small glassed panel
with a brass indicator showing
(both inside and out)
whether the door is locked or free.
This enables anticipation,
especially useful
when the hands are full.

The doorknobs are brass
and do not turn.

9

After two injections
(anaesthetic and muscle-relaxant),
a rubber grip's inserted in the mouth
wedging the teeth;
the temples are then dabbed with paste,
electrodes attached
(trailing wire back
to the small varnished wood box)
and the switch turned.

The body seizes;
mechanical, it overloads.
The scrunched face is centripetal
and the shot forehead
snaking with live-wire veins.
The wishbone spine
strains like a brittle bow
and the limbs hammer.

When it's over,
the body is turned on one side,
dead weight
as if just thrown through a wall,
and wheeled next-door
where curtains are drawn round,
briskly, on shushing rings.

10

My coverlet over me,
blue top, white underside,
that Hokusai wave.

The headlice dream.
But not lice:
small scrunchy bodies
shower into the sink.

Coverlet heaped on my head.
Counterpain.

Making waves.
'Whelmed in deeper gulfs.'
In my father's copy
the man drowning

behind tissue-paper,
one hand help up
to the speck of ship.
'Whelmed in deeper.'
Your finger lifted
and the tissue-paper
curling back on him,
a thin rustle
blurring him.

11

Beyond the chapel,
high firs are clotted with nests.

Resting sheer on stiff wings
like oars paused in water, crows flock over

or muscle upward,
black blazonry jagged on sky.

Two axe down to plump on the aerial
above the TV room.

They break vowels on the roof
then, together, thump off.

Inside, the six o'clock news
breaks into chevrons.

A minute later,
the aerial is still trembling.

12

Bulbs burst yellow
over the walls' glared paint.
The corridor curves and diminishes,
a comet-tail glitter trailing the tug
just passed with its load of laundry
(dirty washing in the white bags,
soiled in the blue).

The corridors boxed with brightness.
There is a smell of tired disinfectant,
a sixty-watt silence.
Night glasses blank windows.
Doorknobs bend a dotted line
to its vanishing-point
brass winks relayed through unused air.

SELIMA HILL

The Notebook (1987)

This is the notebook of someone who had been an inmate for nearly twenty years. We have typed it out as near as possible as we found it.

Ward One
My socks are blood-soaked.
Hattie's mac drips in the cloakroom.
'Dim gradual thinning of the shapeless gloom'
I long to run my fingers down those bannisters
D. has had her renaissance, she says. Have I?
I am shy with sophisticated people, sophisticated with shy
people.
When I think of the long days at the bathroom window . . .
I have dreamt of it three times.
Grapes for supper, I took them outside, I wanted to eat them
in the moonlight, no-one saw.
Running when exams are over.
I have put a map of Paris by my bed.
I am going outside again tonight.
Frosted hay smelling of cows' knees. Boots. Chives.
Molly's bicycle.
I will be sixteen in the night.
If poetry was dangerous . . .
I want to wash my hair. K. is looking at me.
Pain – my hand, the blood. Philosophy of suffering. I am
prepared.
Two parcels, two letters, one post-card, one telegram. Why
have I grown to these four dimensions?
I want a fly to put in my ink.
The man they label little lest one day I dare to grow . . .
the thighs of the warm dark night.

No-one must ever read my poems.

H. has got another photo. I will steal. I will scream. It
is all because of H.

Everything she's got I want.

"Have you ever watched the morning
mounting on the interlines and crosses
Of a bird-abounding mud-plain . . ."

"The Romantic outsider looks for truth; the existentialist
outsider looks for the point of truth."

Il bat sur leur terrain ses plus dangereux concurrents
Medea of Euripides.

Love. The avoidance of this pain is the beginning of wisdom
for it is strong enough to contaminate the whole of our
lives.

Centre partings. Men in brown shoes. Men and women in
jerseys without shirts.

Inability to sustain even the most

Sitting on a stool waiting for justice. For juice.

Absence of God implies need of God

I don't know where I'm going. I need a sense of direction
to get me there.

Still telling me to go to parties but I stay at home writing
essays to myself.

Who saw in death a dark immaculate flower.

Angels do not warm slippers.

Clarkes Perfect Plug.

Painted houses. The fellowship of green grass.

Sur vos lèvres, alors, meurent les Caratines. Sur vos
lèvres, alors, meurent les Caratines.

How many devils can dance on the point of a pin?

The forth of hairwashing water. Loxene Medicated Shampoo.
Your nearest stationer.

Rigor maris mare rutae – Sudden chill with shivering
Married? why only the other day I saw him alive and walking
about.

A German lady with three rings on her red fingers.

Commercial undertaking

The world of passing spaniels.

Because there are no people I say tiles.

Ulster Monarch September 1963. The sound of pouring coal.

The loneliness of harmony.

Do the pears hang in patterns on the tree?

Ivory Coast. Sassandra. Mask in Painted Wood.

The perfect can only arise from the imperfect. Eupedocles.

I dreamt that D. said he had left me, and I tried to
remember how he had kissed me when I arrived, and asked D.
was she **sure**.

Baby's blue plastic plate with mashed potato on.

She was actually giving away the p. she had always loved.

The envelope had been opened. It was full of pictures and
papers. At last she gave it to me.

The captain said it was hardly worth it.

The roads everywhere were blocked.

They told her to use the ladders which had been specially
painted for her by the doctors.

We had to walk through a lighted farm building.

Cheap 7/6 – for Aldermaston Marchers.

Les Amants.

Rime royal has what ottava lacks.

Not so much a fear of going away, as a fear of going on.

If I was completely at one with (nature? beauty?) I wouldn't
write.

Something obscene about young people being rich.

Genet "If my song was beautiful, and has disturbed you, will
you dare to say that he who inspired it was vile?"

Older people do not know they change although they think
they do.

Hope is memory; memory is self-pity.

Beauty in nature is final; beauty in women is only a means to
an end.

Contradiction to use love as a basis for anything.
Not daring to look at men asleep.
I didn't mean any harm.
The black bus conductor who said I was looking kinky.
There was a little one-eyed gunner who killed all the birds
that died that summer.
("With these two hands I've fought my way into the gutter.")
Ayer = Brahms.
The green ribbon. It has no mean. It is the meaning.
The poet is god's spy.
(. . . So happy and if not love than a very strong desire to see
you **now** and agree how right we are! . . .)
My solitude box.
Music pursuing something.
People shouting in the swimming-pool.
J. reads **with stamina**.
Frottir, pas cassir.
Hope D. won't try to contact Sat. Would like to tel. as
soon as poss. because of money.
Amatorcula.
I'm sorry, I don't know where it went wrong.

Ward Two
Now I sleep with anonymous people in dreams.
When I was a little boy I washed my mammy's dishes; I put my
finger in my eye and pulled out little fishes.
I'm your lover than you think.
De Quincey of the skating Wordsworth.
"My hand froze on her neck and I couldn't let go" (boy of 14
to policemen)
(Antique-dealers going to sleep)
      Angor inter arta
      Gurgitum Cacumina
      Gemens alatizo

Intuens morifera

Non conscendens supera

The scaffolding on the building at the station, with men's
shirts hanging from the ends 'Now that I'm a woman' – now
that I am no longer a virgin? Now that I am pregnant. That I
have loved D, that I have loved D and know that I don't love
him anymore? Now that I'm not pregnant any more? That I can read
medieval Latin? That my hair has been cut shorter?

I feel like C's breath when he's got asthma.

Swimming today was like swimming in pins.

New council pigeon lofts.

Dreamland TO LET

Dans le chemin de Madelaine – encore cet immense desir de
depouillement

devant une nature aussi belle que celle la.

the building at the station.

"Not a man, but a cloud in trousers". Who said that?

The window cleaner wanted to have a photograph of his dead
wife, who was ugly, enlarged.

'Perversity which is mine like a hill' Creeley

Knowing someone from the neck up.

Sensible emptiness

"Bearded Kenneth Saunders, 49, from London, has left here
dressed in a white robe and carrying a five-foot aluminium
cross on a white transcontinental walk."

Johnnie Norrie Gaed up three paper stairies and in at a paper
doorie.

Give flowers to the rebels failed.

Teddy Bear and Bassinette 1911.

And two sons run swift roans in the high Summer grass.

Dag Hammarskjold: Never measure the height of a mountain
until you have reached the top, and then you will see how
low it is.

The Irish question has never passed into history because it
has never passed out of Politics.

The fact that I was young.

The astrologer said I would be famous, and I immediately
thought that I would rather go on writing, and that I didn't
want to be famous. My ambition: not to be famous.

Millie earned herself a million copies.

Sleeping with the big boys.

A flat-footed wind-up toucan.

Doing nothing else, like balletomanes.

He took her to the common, and gave her ham sausage.

He came in and moved her toys – tears; and he goes in then
goes out again – tears; he prepares her food but it is not
ready – tears; he puts the cockatoo beside her chair –
tears; he plays her music during her bath – tears.

"As a Swede, reluctantly in exile, I have never known a more
voluntarily imprisoned lot of enlightened men than in this
country. Yet you have got nobody but yourselves to blame . . ."

Full of loving sorrow. I am a young mother **full of loving
sorrow**. Betty told me not to leave her in the sun but I
did.

I sometimes think she is dead.

I am knitting a black rabbit.

I am the mother in the Mother-And-Baby Unit. I have a
discontented "sideways" look.

"But you know they love dancing. The inmates think the
dance is really beautiful."

Spies.

Trixie. Trixie loves sweet tea. She used to ride a horse,
great big one.

Stubbing out her endless cigarettes. Burning someone's eyes
out. "So fucked-up!"

The circulating phosphorescent snort of the night nurse.

attitude ironique et ludique des schizophrenes

The giraffes are really nuns

Cambridge – the streets warm and familiar. Girls sitting in
the Corn Exchange with their handbags on their knees.
R. ate his soup in silence, like a barge being loaded with flour.
G. and I were disappointed we could not go on R's motorbike,
and later G. did.
I am watching the flies on the sugar, which is warm. The
cats are crying for their milk but I will not give it to
them. It's more positive than being merely kind.
'Aghast at such depths of opacity!
I love him at night and in the evening.
The function of art is to create a demand for the complete
satisfaction of which the hour has not yet struck.
The function of art is to show that free choice exists.
Paint peeling in the sun. G. is not yet back. I would not
have been so gently if she had not been so unkind.
A man in a dark suit waving from the back of red sports car.
When we came up out of the subway, the sky was mauve and
heavy and the street was yellow. Yvan said the sky was the
same colour all the time.
A black cat came into the flat. It was as big as a small
dog.
When buying new shoes, we think of everything in terms of
New Shoes.
1. Piano 2. Bed 3. She walks away.
Cats; as if someone has split mercury on the town.
The landlady's son is listening to the wireless.
Anorexia – suffocation by chocolate.

Still half asleep, putting on sandy jerseys.
J. said "Why am I such a good mother?"
We sat on the steps by the pebbly bit while the children
looked for wolves and dolphins by the bathing huts, and S.
went to look for a shop that sells Tampax.
When the crocodile came on, she said **Back home please**

and M. suddenly fell asleep on my knee.

Chocolate biscuits at the Lost Children's Hut.

Bigger. Centipede. Pineapple. Turnips.

The gorilla's house was dark.

I treat her like that because she always seems to be on the verge of tears.

". . .Fate had earmarked me for less compassionate sewers" Molloy.

We never feel cold.

She was found with Daniel across her knee.

As I went by a dyers door/I met a lusty tawny moor/Tawny hands and tawny face/Tawny petticoats/Silver lace.

Waiting for the actors at the Act-In-Tree.

Victorians in Sommer – Nymphenburg.

O lorry, O lorry, O rabbit, O rabbit.

. . . Who won't let them go when they're teenagers.

She cried in the Whale Hall for it but we couldn't get it back.

She doesn't mind. He just spills it.

Just because I don't like doing it, I think I'm not doing it.

Two hens called Phyllis and Violette (carved on the gate of their run).

M (about the baby): I hope he's not thinking about milk all the time. I don't really know if he likes me kissing him or not.

All alone, under the aeroplanes, behind the cries, inside the despair.

A bag of figs, a jug of milk, a Shetland shawl.

Exciting and soothing at the same time, like a tree.

His smiles – like waiting for a slow-dripping tap to drip.

We will all go swimming.

He said he would wish that lots of people had a white horse in their garden.

Berryman's Dream Boys and my book on goats.

Describing her long painful labour: "not a day passes when she does not think of it, but with pleasure!"

Ate chocolate biscuits, fished in the stream with sieves.

It's only polite.

Full of roses and cornflowers.

Short coloured legs sticking out.

The valley is so still. The daisies on the lawn are enormous.

Mint tea and ice-cream./I have nothing.

Going to Cheddar Gorge to pick strawberries. The Strawberry farm. The Strawberry hillside.

Sitting on the sofa in a nice friendly sort of way.

All this is very boring compared to the caravan in the woods.

She slept on the kitchen table next to a basket of strawberries.

Her huge fragile head.

Or here in my bedroom which makes me sad.

They must feel very strange and excited after their long journey.

"Time like an ever-rolling stream bears all her sons away.

They fly forgotten, as a dream dies at the opening day."

A field full of long-legged hares.

The last of the sun makes the grey wood pink.

A fence worn smooth by cows.

They shake their soft square heads.

Ugly, but very very sweet.

I watched him from the diving-board.

"When you want to call him, fat, dear, call him plump. Say plump, it sounds nicer doesn't it dear?"

"The delightful world comes after death and Paradise succeeds the Grave". Browne.

Pounding down the beach and throwing themselves into the

sea. **Plump.**

Standing in my swimsuit on the hot rocks, I couldn't answer.

It seems a bit unkind on the nurse to write it down.

A little lull.

A white funnel, an orange mug, a silver egg-cup.

. . . Playing in the kitchen with the cooks. I knew they
would look after him.

Box.

Ward Three

Miles away from anywhere.

I want to go on writing poems till the last minute.

Zebra Danio. A fish in a tank like a drop of gin.

Synchronized sunbeams.

Tired by happy.

Some, falling faster, stuck with blood.

The tall physicist is rocking. Grapefruit juice.

Unfortunately I am reading Graham Greene.

I was pouring milk onto his cereal: "Quick, quick, or the
milk will go sour."

I sleep curled up like a shrimp

She died in the best hospital,

staring at the cold equipment.

"I long for scenes where man hath never trod."

Also, I am going to Moscow.

'Third World Women And Lesbians Simmer."

My mother is crumbling away like a biscuit.

At least he's clean.

Do not console me. I am not your friend.

After the long night will come the long and terrifying day.

He does not know he needs me pale myself to insignificance.

A less soft but a straighter whiteness in the air.

Mother water, I am your baby.

A whole string of questions. A bedside light.

2% of married couples make love on the stairs.

Now snow is filling up his little head.
the yellow flip-flap of the albatross.
Like a butcher, deep in rubber buckets of defrosting blood,
tearing the hearts from cows.
Percy, my grand-mother's spider.
You never lift a finger,
Bred to weep. A tiny sunlit bone.
Stuck in one position like a model figurine.
Her answering call.
He was painting croquet balls for his mother-in-law.
The little boy I thought you were teaching to swim.
A young girl sitting on a gate, barbed wire between her
legs.
Flat on his face.
Edith Södergran would not drink the milk the neighbours
brought because they killed her cats who had been mousing in
the night across the border.
Illuminated gloves.
He was the shyest man I had ever met.
It was all just a wonderful dream.
The Canary Man.
I wish I was a warm friendly person.
I want you to buy the boots **very** much.
I wonder why the seagull has such a dirty tummy. Let's go
home.

Larne – Stranraer. It sends a shiver
Everybody said so.
A strawberry blonde. A famous boxer gave her chocolates.
Doing cartwheels with nothing on under my skirt
Her father slept in the stables because he wanted to be with
his horses as much as possible.
As soon as she walked in at the door, her mother knew she
wasn't a virgin any more.

Blue Grass. Simon Dee. Dreams of getting married.

It was very difficult for us, but you were very patient.

He was hoping Minty would **draw him towards her** in the same way.

That's what they're like, my two sisters.

My socks were bloodsoaked.

We thank her as we leave, and she nods, but doesn't look up.

... whose sheets, even now, are being turned down for you ...

She is the woman who runs the shop in the hospital. I am the patient.

The man who thinks he's a bird smokes Embassy cigarettes.

Put your empty packets in the bin, Reggie.

The nun is wearing her yellow and black striped shirt.

Bits of vegetable in soup – nipples.

When the train moves off, and I mouth "Good-bye", she picks up her paper and methodically starts to cry.

My father's wool cardigan.

A wasp settled on his chin. He tip-toed to the sink, turned on the taps, and shook the wasp into the water.

Far out the lonely golfers start to cry ...

A girl with a duck on her lap.

A chocolate elephant waving from a shop window.

Gertrude Bell's linen-covered thighs.

Ships fan out towards Europe.

Running over the Jebel Druze ... Eating mulberries.

Van Gogh – his ear cut off like a sprout. Dropping it in boiling water.

The old lady at the farm – he thought they were her boots, but they were knitted socks.

Cutting her nails and watching them jump across the room like fleas.

They're thinking of Anna, how nice and thin she is.

Girls in wet T-shirts like fruit ripening in plastic bags.
Washing cherries.
What's she doing? She's crying.
It's not me. She forgot about the trains. It's time.
"It's absolutely true – they eat white men, when they
haven't got baboons. Ha ha."
He thought he was a goose.
The airport at Sophia is a tin shed.
The lecturer in archaeology can talk for exactly sixty
minutes.
We wanted to explore the Brahmaputra incognito.
I got home at 5 in the morning and my stocking was still
empty.
The driver is going so fast they get squashed at every corner.
Beaded whisks of elephant tails to swat fat African flies.
Just us, and our yurts, and a few cows.
It's not you I'm thinking of – it's Frank.
Slices of frozen heart.
How you want to be with me always, how you hate the snow . . .
The fields are flooded and full of paddling ducks. The
doctor is reading **Peer Gynt** by the fire.
The three doctors had a meal for £149.
Trying to warm his balls on a hot-water bottle.
Wales is snowbound – drifts of snow, frozen lakes, horses
galloping into the snowy windy.
There is a sort of exercise in happiness going round – Think
of the Happiest Moment of Your Day. Also, Your Ideal Day
Out.
An aeroplane hit a bridge and sent cars and plane crashing
into the Potamac – ice, wet tights, buckled metal. Screams
and cries.
In Washington there are long queues for bits of cheese.
We sat by the fire eating tangerines.
Cutting back the privet.
She does too much.

People are saying it will snow again.

The nurse: "I will save my sparkle for my work and, if I can make it stretch." (can sparkle stretch?) "for the evenings".

He says he always hates the girls he's made love to.

The sound of rain splashing on the siren. The Psychiatric Unit on the bank.

Keep offering me apples, which I hate.

The red-haired nurse spent all day in O.T. today although she was off duty.

Always the same advice: Cut it dead.

In my dream, I was in America crying and crying and crying.

"That's the trouble with C, she always wants to be dropped somewhere . . ."

The smell of Guinness from the Guinness factory, merging with the smell of rhinos from the zoo.

A story – I haven't been able to think of one all my life.

Enormous jerseys and no trousers.

Ashes, hazels, sheep. Crystallized rose-petals.

Station Road – Stations of the cross – Scratching himself like a dog.

When I am feeling happy, other people think I am unhappy.

T. lying in bed with two jerseys on and two bars on the fire, reading my books.

Rock, dry grass, pain.

She said 'I know what C. and I will talk about on our way to school'.

We watched some moorhens walking about in some trees, their big green feet like camels!

The day seem to pass in slow jerks, as if I was watching it.

They got dressed straight into their swimming things.

Spends most of the time asleep or carrying bags.

Her little silk figure disappearing under the magnolias.

The geese in the twilight. Builders in the house.

During the Aikodo Demonstration someone collapsed in the row
behind me.
Feeble-minded. I've been brought up to think of people like
him as feeble-minded.
Crisps and hat blowing in the wind.
Just a wave in a particle-less, mysteriously conscious
universe.
I wish they would all go away.

T. noticed that I am suddenly very argumentative.
Physical stiffness dissolving in smooth radiating coils as I
walk along in the fresh air.
Banded snails on a saucer.
I am sorry if his loving me means that he will miss me.
There are still pigs in the shed. (Later: the pig died in
the shed).
Dreamt R and A's baby had a period – blood on the nappy,
Rabbits, primroses, herons, peewits, swans.
He stayed to enumerate the muggings.
Coming to no conclusions.
The final, domestic sound of milk bottles being put out.
While the children have gone upstairs, they have not gone to
bed (how we used to have to translate Latin.)
My socks were bloodstained.
The cars constantly passing the day-room window exhaust me.
Beckett's
"First Love"; pigs in warm earth; gold; orgasms;
kedgeree.
The bluebells in the 2 gardens next door shine with an angry
violet light.
The same man who said he liked my cardigan.
Motor-bike helmets like wood-peckers' skulls. The jarring.
I wear my new jersey every day.
At V's house – martini, peanuts, mirrors. I felt like foam
rubber (or is it 'my illness'?)

He has cut into the chicken's gall bladder.

The go-back-and-kill-your-grandfather paradox.

Walking across the hospital lawn, enacting memories for the future.

Quantum physics, fairy cakes, ice-cubes.

Although they were in Bethlehem.

Billy Fury dies in his sleep.

> Dolomite, alabaster, obsidian, jasper, malachite
> garnet, turquoise, gold, quartzite, granite,
> lapis lazuli, faience, butter-scotch.

James Wolfe, Victor of Quebec.

Eyes inlaid with glass

Its vaulted lid

Ife; Owo; Igbo-okwu; Nok.

If you can't ride two horses at once, you shouldn't be in the circus.

What did he mean? And why did the other man say **I thought you had gone yes gone?**

The warm vending machine. The dangerous gorilla.

Rocks – vocal – give sweet instruction.

The shaggy remains of a star.

Singing, and hearing in her mind James Joyce' voice singing above hers.

Massed Ascensions. Massed Boy Scouts.

A pig on its hind legs covering its eyes.

Shade trees – a coolness – dwo

Parading vast bunches of keys.

Pawning gold.

I want to scream and scream and scream and all I do is write.

I want to scream and scream and scream down in my book.

(A peaceful evening) the sort I've been married so long for.

Father coming home like the ride coming in.

Darwin: the bare living on blue water

Autumn Antics

Seafaring man,
Portable hen.
Banked
jiggle
tart
One word. Enclosed by hate.
I feel like string.
Painting in the blue. Bring out your long blue sentences
like trains.
Apricot jam, apricot ice cream, Grizzly bars 'with apricot',
A message: **Apricots** Abrecock. Albarcoque. Sunning himself,
my darling, on a rock. Praecos – it's so early. They're
going to mow me down.
The roof of my mouth is aching – to get away from the
kissing – Tears rise up like milk through the thin tubes of
the early morning milking machine.
He had written: **I know I can rely on you absolutely.**
The movement of planets, the alternation of tides.
Death is willed.
The well-known concept of the sky as cow.
Primeval hill.
The Cannibal hyena, a fresh wind.
Natural gradual in her processes.
The redoubtable Ngoni
Hooks and lines are used by small boys and men.
The eyes move under closed lids.
The King – gracious and terrible.
The waiting-room. It frightens me.

The humble mole.
The Festival of the Staircase.
Diseases of the Mind – Ravishing – Nurseryman – Bloated –
Faith-healer – Polo – Ceylon – Pet monkey – Bungalow – as if
they were lovers – Tick tick tick
Gongs, bowstands, diadems and umbrellas

I feel better when I say I keep bees.

Snow on the paths. Mary was followed by a troupe of giant hens.

Fun – something Americans can't see beyond nothing if not uncomplaining.

Ice-floe floe floe

Fly whisks of lion and zebra tails.

His or her personal stool is blackened with soot and the blood and fat of sacrificial sheep.

Wild bees' nests.

Sufficient unto the day is the joy thereof.

No visitors.

No snowflake falls in the wrong place.

The aim of the course is to make them feel like string.

"All my life I've longed to crawl along the ground with a gun . . ."

A secret bag of maple walnuts. Crocodiles.

"A fly got stuck in my painting" (in O.T.)

Granny moving deeper and deeper into the pink and purple trees.

Lop-eared rabbits, bananas, little cakes.

Obviously very fond of her.

The day passed all too soon.

The secret of multiple walnuts.

The swelling is as big as a peach.

Wearing big boots and shorts.

(God) controlling the world but not the universe.

Scotch pines, weasels on the gated road. The little dog was limping.

The bits about eating meat, not the bits about fairies.

A Spaniel called Tony. D. was wonderful!

I like the way you sound so breathless – it's so erotic.

Get me another dog, would you?

One frantic snow-storm.

Kok's date-like hands.

'Snow on the paths. Mary was followed by a troupe of giant hens.' When I say Mary, it's me!

All to myself! as lazy and grumpy as a king.

Beaches, cows, boats.

People who try and leave London will be shot.

'I said when I was at the hospital I kept hearing voices."

Antibiotics. Sleet.

Mothercare tights. Private happiness. Jiving to Elvis till 4.00.

It's already dirty.

Mrs. Holly praised by 'fortitude'.

'Trying to achieve that blissful state in which you don't know where you are."

What Peter calls 'high spirits'.

Unsatisfied by streams of friends, I wish I was riding a horse.

"... to get a little carpet in our bedroom, to go under the door, which will need to be a little bit planed down ..."

Sadder than intended. Blood, tomatoes, a woman crying.

"As long as you're happy, it's OK." **A Whiter Shade of Pale.**

More apologies.

He is applying for a job at the swimming pool.

Beside a bowlful of stones.

Gazing out of the window in the middle of the day.

On their way to catch their train home. Ginger-biscuits. A hair-dryer.

"I pity his poor wife."

If they are not careful, and if they do not work or pray.

He sits in the dark chewing his fingers.

It was dark by the time we got home.

I can't read any of them ... "inability to concentrate" ...

voices I keep hearing all the time ...

Washed-out, quiet and affectionate.

'Obviously very sick.'

A mohair cardigan, a bowl of pears.

Yes, she said, **the structure of one's day.**

Playing Scrabble by the heater, Heather winning as usual.

My poor face is aching.

Her poor face is aching.

". . . the feeling one comes away with . . ."

Her goldfish, her villanelle, her big baggy jumper.

She said she was a good parrot.

Ducks and figs. The dry white grass.

Crows, hyacinths, a man mending a roof.

Accept what I mean to myself.

He lay on the airbed saying he had had a head-ache for
eleven years.

Ward Four

I go to the pinewoods in my dreams.

Green streamers, a goose. Is the dining-room very shabby?
A boat called Wilfred.

My bottom feels cold and dirty.

Gazing over sunlit fields

"Sorry if I sound patronizing . . ." ". . . Keep hearing voices
. . ." ". . .and pulled up my nightdress in a great handful
like THIS!"

Red cherry lollipops on green sticks.

Paths padded with sand. White espadrilles. Potatoes.
Women Saints.

It's 4.00. The rabbit's wide awake.

Very erotic dreamy night. Kisses after kisses.

All the lost baby's family are missing. Her carricot was
floating in the sea.

He is on his knees in the garden, clipping grass.

People say it's all so free, so honest.

A pet rook.

A beautiful green Portuguese Laurel.

"Surely he doesn't need a **new car!**"

A suitcase full of bread and jam, like this.

Out late playing the ball.

The funeral director's black car screeching round the corner – suddenly free to go as fast as he wants.

My mother's outing – walking through the artificial jungle with her daughter, me.

Breast-milk. Secrets. I've got no legs.

Wrapped in blankets in an enormous room. Trying to get an orgasm by meditating.

The Eternal Now. Awareness with comment.

Cushions – tea – jelly – getting angry.

Mountain fastnesses – the queen fish.

That beautiful sentence aches in the back of my throat – The busy bee hath no time for sorrow.

Ice. Toothache. Smoking.

She lay in the sun on a tussock.

Six summer puddings with red roses on top, tents of almost white canvas, broad beans, her dress of creamy satin.

Slow, slow, slow. Doesn't come. He eats dead fish.

I don't' know how I got there, or if anyone knew I was there.

The walls were apple-green. The man said **You're schizophrenic**.

The feeling of the nurses' hands on my arms. I'm blind.

The corner of the day-room shines like coal. I'm terrified.

Joyce is very fat and comes from Wales.

Everyone lives in hospitals, she said.

No time for sorrow.

She seemed neither sad nor happy.

I am sorry I never loved her.

The waiting room. The humble mole.

I don't remember eating or drinking.

A black plastic pig with a chewed head, about the size of a walnut.

Soon I'll be better, then I'll be good.
I am warm. I am not in any kind of pain.
My socks are bloodsoaked.
"Of course, I couldn't bear to read it – it was like going
into a sick-room!"
The habit of superiority.
I was glad it was late.
"Strolled" across the beach to the aquarium.
Lait de bronzage. The Baboon In Fact and Legend.
Melting moments.
The wooden weather-man: Bow-bow-bow, Knock-Knock-Knock.
"And how was he to know? – he lives in another world."
From the patients' kitchen: "Not **up – down!**" and the sound
of someone crying. It's Michelle.
'Our' gulls.
My cushion smells of wallflowers.
If she had fallen over, I would have tried to comort her.
He says he's been depressed since 1941. Snowflakes and
cathedrals. Super-String.
Defoe's desparate something.
Sister: "Everyone admires our Christmas Tree!"
Everything he does is wrong.
He says everything he does is wrong.
His desperate (something) for honesty.
Sausage, chips and peas, and apple crumble.
His desperate bid for honesty.
Coffee and pet-food and the final proofs.
I remember the good times.
The other dog bit his paw. (This was the same dog that
later killed him.)
The rich girl's father is going to take her away because of
her bloodsoaked socks.

The white team's players, the orange flowers, the smell of
pine.

Fleabane, Shrimps, stiff salty hair.

Bleached wood stamped Rotterdam. The Whitsun outing.

"I've got happiness! Where? In my heart ..."

Periwinkles and green crabs.

Fried egg at sunset.

The clock has just struck 11. It is 7 o'clock.

Macaroni and Marrow Chesse Pie.

The rocks, spotted by rain, like sleeping leopards, soften.

The stillness of collapsed stars.

I am surrounded by happy birds and beetles.

The doctors block the corridors.

Red sausages, grasshoppers, tramps.

Fat hands and rocking horses fill the sky.

"I **could** be busy all the time, but what I would be doing
would be so boring."

Himalayan pig-peg game. Cocky-Olly.

The seeds of the red-centred sunflowers came from Paris.

"Something to do with his willie ..."

I do not need a coat. Leave me alone.

He stayed in bed reading "Monsters Of The Deep".

On the tip of a turquoise diving-board. Not Methadone.

Grey juvenile flamingos. Ravioli with cream.

All I want to do is say I hate him.

Worshipping God in a garden. Going for little journeys.

Sitting under the oak-tree eating a sandwich.

Love seems so personal and fiddly.

Fences, mud, leather gloves.

Grey juvenile fingers.

Seeing myself as a little passionate nun.

It casts a faint shadow on the white road.

Mushrooms, herons, woolly bears. My mother.

She called her terrapins Tight Perm and Three Volts (It's true!)

Answering that question brings the – and the – and the – ...

Towels, baskets, stew, and a tender young monkey-puzzle
tree.

Lost in the mists of time!

Apricot pudding, buckets of coal, the 'scenery'.

I have had my horizons broadened by the young doctor –
Whitebeam, cigarettes, a potted plant. His wife said 'When
they were little . . ."

Alternately crying and reading.

A grey T-shirt showing under the black one in a way that
doesn't make it clear if it's intentional or not.

Nakedness in unfamiliar places.

I wanted to release the ravens. I felt I nearly was going
to. The voluntary worker's full skirt.

Salopettes from Bunny. Eight little vegetable tarts.

Patrick's efficient packing in Nicola's detached house.

Cigars, church, two shining bathrooms. **The poor girls' got
to see the doctor again.**

Knitting while the lamb is roasting.

A three-hour walk with Ricky. Rubbing and polishing stones.
Stones – complete and lasting.

It's happened already – and I can't believe it!

I must look up! I must look up!

A three-hour walk – and he thought the dog was dead!
Seeing myself as a little passionate man.

(I had to cross the corner of the day-room). Hands, bowls,
footsteps, padded orange.

Something rhythmical, like swimming. The Black Stone of
Mecca.

Forehead-Smashers. It's happening again already.

Silently a hare foraged over soggy islands of fruit.

The most intelligible passages. Coal. Contrasting coal
with milk jelly.

I dread the human voice.

I am the roller of socks.

If I open my eyes, the orange might come, trembling and bright.

Hands, bowls, footsteps, padded orange. Somebody calling my
name.

If they've got holes in their socks, I have to go and cut
their nails. (Please cut **the space round the nails** and not
the nails themselves.)
The doctor squirting juice into my eyes.
Two children and a dog run out of the house and up the steep
hill. They zigzag over the white grass. One of them
suddenly throws quicklime into the eyes of the other one,
who is taken away to London. **Hospital for you.**
We felt no sympathy or joy. We didn't play those games.
Who gave me food, and washed my clothes, and talked to all
my friends?
I thought I was called Mary too, but I didn't say anything.
Keeping whisky under her bed.
Paddling in the sea with her stockings on.
She's called Patricia.
I think she kept the bottle in a box.
A bowl of cornflakes. A shower of sugar. She is the
Sister. The tumbling orange will come.
She is the Sister.
She has an erotic zone.

Slug so small, erotic-zone-less, crawl. **But even the slug
has public hairs, you know.**
I think I have swallowed a puppy. It keeps me awake at
night.
Reflections in still water. Do you think that's right?
Someone has painted my movements. When I move, I'm red. As
thick as ox-blood and gravy! (The porter eats it with his
bare hands.) (I saw him eating in the library again.)
("Come on, Reggie!")

The hospital is underwater. We are swimming to the water-
green Dispensary.

The hospital is underwater. The doctors' coats are green.
TO WIDEN BRAINS, NAIL JOINTS LOOSELY.

This little thing's been homeless for so long.

Soon I will die, soon the twinklies will come.

The water in the bath goes waaa – waaa – waaa.

SHELDON FLORY

Halfway Pond (1989)

To my brother John with Alzheimer's

Look, the ducks are back. See,
the buffleheads scoot back and
forth in their turbans; the merganser drake
bobs in his glossy green jacket and
white shirtfront, skinny wives
running after, their henna'd hair
frantic.
   We began losing you
ten years ago among
     the pitch-
pine, the scrub-oak and sweetfern
as,
 driving,
   one notices
how radio stations un-
focus, then flake apart in
the air behind.
    Your grammarian's kit
lies strewn across the grown-
over garden: pronouns, referents,
subjects, objects
     tangle and
untangle.
   Insubordinate cat-
briar creeps back across
fire-blackened sand forced
once, by kitchen offal buried
daily, to become soil.

                    Where
are your Resolveds, your rebuttals, now?
the trump cards, the dread puns?
Sunk with your killer drop-shot where
the horned pout and pickerel lie up
on the dark side of the island.

The ends of your sentences, whole
questions – fateful, invisible – hang
over the dark red bogs between
here and Bloody Pond.

Ducks dive, come up
empty, fly on
North.

JACQUELINE BROWN

Thinking Egg (1991)

Eggs are full of life containing nutrients, proteins, fats,
vitamins, minerals and a tiny pocket of air – nearly everything
essential for living.

(Delia Smith's Cookery Course, Part One)

Particular

Palm size, shaped to hand,
so light a burden
cold from the kitchen
rough gritskin puckering thumbtip,
iridescent smear of stuck straw
a skid of farmyard muck or henshit.

Baby Egg

Last egg, offering nearly everything
essential to life in a baby's hand.
First baby, topheavy bandy but willing
to lurch from Auntie to Mother, bearing
the last egg of the ration. Mother's memory
of egg. Not mine.
A tale plucked from the scarce heap of story
retained to niggle questions. What
possessed them? What mischief governed
such a gamble with only egg? Oooh-ooh
the lifted breath as one foot rears
tremors   finds earth   Aaaaah as
hand swivels   stays   rights itself.
That's right.   Clever baby.   Bring the egg.

What was in the four blue eyes?
Not my memory. A blank.
Eyes of the sisters are ash now. Egg
in my hand to break and cook and eat.
The palm contracts.
Crushed egg slimes between joints and knuckles,
cauls the boat of the hand like sperm or snot.

In the Room (I)

Come too late to see
the eyes someone's
thumbed shut.
Anger like shutters
slamming,
pity slicking the throat,
the nasal membrane swells,
oozes; tears are furious
hot.
Not for her. She's gone.
This one's for me.
That dreadful shift of face
from quick to this,
to dirty tallow,
yolk-eyes filmed over
by solid cataracts of skin,
these cheeks landslipped
from nose, no lips,
under the tautened sheet
how flat, how shrunk –
blown shell, husk.
Windows shut. Curtains still.
Is it temper that so stirs air?
Does air move of itself?
Or is it longing that rucks

the bedclothes
that lets the sign go out?

A nurse says, *ashes and urns and years later . . it's just sometimes*
the newly-dead don't lie still, seem to live for a moment, move
slightly, sigh or fart as a tiny pocket of air escapes.

Egg-Gathering with Lily

Nan, fat as the butter she spreads so lavish
melting the toast to yellow finger-smears.
Holiday Nan, uncorseted and featherbed muzzy,
slurring her slippers from table to stove
black pan atilt in her hand, egg an island
in limpid fat, edges all wave-bitten lace.

Godda feed you up a bit. Skinny Min.
Get you strong. Eat up. Good girl.
Egg's good for you. Eggs is meat.

Warrior Nan in her pinny with her zinc bucket
shield that swings and chimes the time it takes
to walk between backstep and henhouse, the last
fat forkful and the fright of feathers.
Skinny Min unwilling to fight the weight of hen,
eyes shut tight against beakstab and flutter,
throat closed down on the pressure of hot egg
on palm. *That's right. Clever girl. Careful.*
Put the egg in the bucket.

Naming of Cuckoo

Outside it's beginning to be almost spring
            inside girl in a gymslip, a blouse,
            a bodice, a vest, brown flannel

                    knickers, ankle socks, laceup shoes;
                    girl at a desk

invisibly trees heave up their tons of water

                    girl in a classroom listening and
                    learning the habits of Cuckoo while
                    brown flannel rusts orange absorbing
                    her failed egg

leaves on the flooding trees are only potential

                    girl writes in an orange-backed notebook
                    Cuculinae – underlined – *Migration*
                    – underlined, altered: *Migratory*
                    Route

windows sting as May alters; becomes April; alters

                    arrows track her traced map – bird
                    prints northward from Africa, north
                    to Europe to here where she's learning
                    Cuculinae built no nests

near-spring leans on the windows, wanting in

                    teacher's breasts are cradled eggs
                    in nylon cups, vest, nylon slip
                    and blouse . . . teacher dictates: –
                    parasitic. . polymorphic. . mimetic eggs

Outside something not-quite mimes authentic spring

                    girl understands: she is a good girl,
                    a clever girl and her secret eggs are hidden,

safe as houses against predation –
nor springs nor cuckoos can frighten her.

Yesterday When I was Young

The morning after *La Ronde* at the Cine
on the Boulevard de Batignolles
he is feeding me soft-boiled egg
from a tarnished spoon. His eyes are freckle
brown, my lips are light pink and open
like a chick's and his are open too, sympathetic.

Look how artfully while he was busy
boiling I've draped the grey sheet.
Look how languidly while he's feeding me
egg I stroke his sculpted lip with one
pink finger, not smiling, trying for
the authentic smoulder.

Charles Aznavour on the turntable caresses
the air, his syllables so controlled and quick
like tongue-flicks all over my bare shoulders,
my artful, part-covered breasts – *Hier encore
j'avais vingt ans, je caressais le temps,
j'ai joué de la vie...*

Were he to open them the French windows
would open inwards, the beige books discover
fat ragged pages that I understand. *Le Monde*
lies wrecked on the floor, his door has a foreign
locking system that I comprehend. I can stand
the foreign consistency of his *oeufs mollets*

and Aznavour's tremolo is doing unmentionable
things to my sheet covered crevices, my lips

are crinkling, and frightened tutting Mother
with her talk of darkened doorsteps and ignorance
of what the world is coming to is miles and
a stretch of sea and miles away.

and *hier encore j'avais vingt ans* but today
I'm Jeanne Moreau and Catherine Deneuve and Bardot
all rolled into one and it's 17th of January 1964
and I'm twenty-one and in Paris and I've found
the authentic vie... Oh, I love myself so much
at this moment, I could eat me.

Egg Woman at her Wedding

She comes in a range of colours
from milkwhite through bisque
and biscuit to a warm honey brown
though her contents are identical.
Her size may vary though the categories
are arbitrary – small, medium, standard,
large, numbered one to seven.
She is always symmetrical, always smooth,
always perfect for holding in the cup
of a hand.
At this moment she is white medium, size 4.
She has been candled for quality – the light
has detected no crack or blemish.

Someone has drawn a face on her –
two circles for eyes, two pinprick dots
for nose, a widened U for a mouth.
This face is innocent and complacent.
She looks almost sly.
She is so sure of her perfection.

She cannot know it cannot last.
When she is held safe in the handcup
she cannot foresee the moment
she will be cracked and eaten,
or the worse moment when somebody
– this boy, maybe, or a robber man –
will prick her either end
with a fine needle and blow her goodness
till her smooth fine features
will hide nothing. Unless a tiny pocket
of air can be called something.

*A truly authentic Coq au vin is made, obviously, with a cock-bird and some
of the blood goes into the sauce, which, by the time it reaches the table, is a
rich, almost black colour.*

(Delia Smith's Cookery Course, Part 2)

Coq au vin

The flat is painted white as a cell
white as the inside of a shell

the marks are tentative yet – preliminary. .
they're learning something of all that's essential
for living together; how to sidestep slightly
to avoid collision and cracking, how to come close
without cracking in the hot bed –
the bed grows wider, larger, till there's room for more
and more: sometimes the empty margins oppress. . but
nothing so simple as to people them *There's M and A
and C and N and B and J – we'll entertain – we'll stun
them with French cuisine*

so down to the market . . she didn't know he loves markets,
his voice rises – she hears *fresh   raw   exciting*

at the meat stall he does all the talking (not mentioning
cocks of course for the butcher is loud and lewd
and over the slant belly his apron's stiff with blood)

plucked and sagging boiling-fowl hang long and flat,
off white like overused lard, like a morning face
stippled blue with small sharp shards of barb,
heads, legs, claws lolling, still coloured in
like the start of a painting

can't not look as butcher cleavers them off, tosses them
to an invisible bin. . . butcher's hair is slick and black
like his dead Dad's. . . butcher's fingers are thick and white:
butcher narrows eyes at her past his eyes . . winks
That's right, chuck, long and slow, lo o ong and slow

the white kitchen, the body slumped on the formica
You must do it. . . . but she can't not watch his hand,
his wrist deep in the flesh, then slurping out guts
and hundreds, thousands of tiny red eggs, potential
eggs – not laughing, his hair as black as his Dad's

far too young for the truly authentic, two of them
retching into the sink, binning the corpse,
drinking the burgundy, ringing the takeaway. .
their bile becomes one bile sliming the plug, and the plughole
two pairs of eyes squint right past each other into dark.

In The Room (2)

On a blue paper sheeting
a woman is lying
on her side, knees to nose
like an ovenready chicken

another woman is stroking
her hand clenched till skin
feels close to tearing, like
she's a baby like she's a child

Just relax if you can
Clever girl that's right

a man in a clean white coat's
an invisible voice moving
unseen in the greenpaint room
just a paper rustle, a mumble

she is not a clever girl
she is not a good girl
the snap of the rubber glove
condemns; the blue paper rucks
with her guilt

under a rubber membrance fingers
inquire, tamper – slick fingers
with no face eyes colour hair –
she has unbodied his fingers

Try to relax   it'll hurt less

a woman is severing a body into bits
guillotine snaps and the head floats
free, snap and snap through the pubic
bone and the body rises, next the legs;
on the blue paper sheet is a tiny pocket
of air encased in stoneskin and a wet
finger learning something and a mind
recording   determined to forget

Try to relax   it'll hurt less

a woman is severing a body into bits
guillotine snaps and the head floats
free, snap and snap through the pubic
bone and the body rises, next the legs;
on the blue paper sheet is a tiny pocket
of air encase in stoneskin and a wet
finger learning something and a mind
recording   determined to forget

the other woman is helping her from the bed
saying *It's all right, it's all over,*
saying *There, dear...* but the silly eyes
can't not look at the map of Africa
damp-etched on the blue paper sheeting
can't not fast forward to all the miles
and miles to go . . desert and sea
and desert and sea before the ghost
of a landing

Fairy Tale

There are trees. She slinks
among them with an empty belly.
There is a house that is bursting
with kids. The kids' mother
has gone off shopping. She is a bad mother,
leaving her kids thus. She would
not miss a kid. One soft milky
kid less would mean nothing to her.

A story mothers read to children
before sleeping, starting *Once
upon a time,* starting like memory

at no-date, no-place, no-time.

There is a door. She knocks on the door
raprap, pleading for, wanting in.
But the kids are good kids.
The kids are clever kids.
The kids are wise in the ways of tales.
They demand to see her fingers,
Dipped in flour, her fingers are white
as a mother's, white as a nanny's.

You can imagine it from their point of view –
the sneck lifted, the flurry, the panicky cries,
their sharp hooves' scatter. . .
a memory they'll consign to blankness,
to a hot dark they can only grope after.

Look how her belly has swollen now.
Look at the silly content smile as she sleeps.
Imagine her point of view when she wakens
in the black of the well-shaft, the pinpoint sky
that could be a million miles away
and her belly packed to bursting with stones.

Poaching

You could assemble a whole catalogue of 'do's and don'ts' on
the subject of poaching eggs . . . Don't attempt to poach more
than two unless you're a really experienced hand.

(Delia Smith's Cookery Course, Part I)

She has heard the women whispering
in hospital rooms of suffering,
pain, blood.

She has stood palefaced in the margins
looking and listening, separate
from them.

While they slept, she has walked in her head
through the bluelit quiet ward, skirting
the nurse,

toe-stepped along to the white corridor,
keeping to walls, to where milky kids
snuffle;

she's walked further to a flurried place
where infants lie flat under glass, taped
to tubes.

Sleepwalking, she has understood theft,
the urge to prise open, steal and hide,
not care

that another woman is crying somewhere
just so long as her own boat of arms
is full.

In the Room (3)

In the dayroom the woman is sitting,
back to the TV, watching the wall.
The woman's body is rocking
forward back, forward back,
ticktock ticktock.
Fragments of song
dribble from her mouth.
If anyone were listening

they'd hear *chicken   egg baby* then
half-audible runs of wordless tune.

No-one is listening.

If the woman were to turn
anyone watching would see
how each cupped palm cradles an elbow
holds it still against the body's motion.
Anyone looking would see a stone oval
where the face should be, two blobs
of blue glass at its widest point.

No-one is looking.

If Stoneface were to rotate
from yellow wall to direct light
the blue glass blobs would see spring
framed in the window – a green lawn
spattered with dandelions,
a horsechestnut bursting,
a sky brailed with birds.

She will not turn.

If anyone were recording the scene
nothing would happen –
back-view of a to-fro rocking woman,
tiny clutches of song
pan-out to yellow walls
a yolk-spattered lawn
pan-in to a black and white TV.

No-one is recording.

No-one has the technology
to record the clackclack
of a mind speedshuttling
woof across frayed warp
weaving what may turn out to be
a cradle-cloth or winding sheet,

no-one knows.

Scrambled

it's dark   don't like the dark
sing a song make the dark go away
look what they've done to my song, Ma
lalalalalalala must've done wrong
bad egg   cracked egg   smacksmacksmack
poor egg   poor hen   Humpty Dumpty Dad
in bits and pieces all the King's horses
and all the King's men can't put Humpty
together again "puir wee hen" says Humpty
when baby stumbles and tumbles   when the bough
breaks   puir wee hen when when when will you lay
me an egg for my tea? Not a stone egg   Silly
hen   Bad hen   smacksmack   sticks and stones
will break my bones   chop off her head.
The blood's all red
look what they've done to my brain, Ma
they've picked it like a chicken-bone
and chickchickchickchick çhicken Run quick
cradle's falling Ma catch Baby Bunting
fetch Daddy   Daddy's gone a hunting somebody
catch her too late   can't put her together
again   say something

Bye Baby Bunting   bye baby   baby doesn't
like the dark   sing song make dark go away

Analytic Egg (1)

Cold room. A woman's voice is telling stories,
tales whose essential truths she's clutching for.
This tale is about Easter in another country –
people who crack red eggs saying Xpiotos áveoty!
saying *He is risen indeed!*

And yet in here – the man's voice is disembodied,
low, issuing from behind her back – *In here, you
refuse this resurrection.* Hate slimes her palms.
She'll smear his telltruth mouth shut with albumen.
Don't speak again. Hug your stories close, safe,
till the hour ends.

Nights, she dreams he is her lover. His penis
is pure white and erect as a pointed finger.
She bears his child, that sits on her immaculate lap,
the two of them hieratic in a yellow gold ellipse
like an icon.

Note: Xpiotos áveoty   Christ is risen

Analytic Egg (2)

grasped   words are just instruments –
scalpels surgical scissors cotton swabs –
tools to help dissect the mind

sometimes her fingers slippy with blood
she'll clumsy a tool and drop it – then
he'll slap another into her palm

under the white masks their eyes don't meet
they don't converse   raprap go their voices
purposeful intent in the quiet room

If you commit yourself here the man's voice says
(Oh she is committed) *we might make a baby*
and it might be fine and it might be dead

something sharp and steely clatters from her hand
the neighbour's baby displayed on the sideboard
the narrow nasty yellow box women-whispers

she remembers stains on the cottonwool
plugging its nostrils   the candle face
above a white frilled cover

where she comes from you must touch
the dead – she tells him of the fist
her fingers made refusing

now she holds out her hand flat
as though for caning   this time
he gentles the knife into it

Theatre

Two glass circles in the door. No real
windows. The room is all hard light.
On the steel table a woman is lying
flat on her back with closed eyes.

A man is feeding her air.
Another man is making a slit in her skin
parting the fat and muscle
just below her belly's swell.

His hands are the colour of corpse
in surgical gloves but quick and deft.
He is reaching into her body.
He is removing a part of her.

Now he is sewing up the flesh
with small neat stitches –
snapsnap go the scissors
as the thread's snipped off.

There are seventeen black stitches
like a line of barbed wire
just above the pubic bone, behind them
a pear shaped pocket of air.

The woman sees none of this.
Her recording mind is whirring
useless in a deep black gap.
It will be of someone else's memory.

Here is waking in another room
wrapped from neck to toe in tinfoil
and the dark-haired man's joke
about a chicken ready for roasting.

She remembers the wobble in his laugh
and the way his eyes try to meet hers,
almost succeed, till lozenges of reflected
silver foil get in the way.

Cuckoo Calling

If she could feel, spring would appal
the world running its egg-and-sperm race
the birdcall blatant with demand.

She is stone: black; heavy; inert.
Where flesh was, moss grows.
Where hope was there is a gap.

In the gap the cuckoo came calling
a flap of wing among trees
and fast and unseen filled it.

At the Garden Centre

The garden-centre son is a bird man,
foster-father to falcons he's reared
from eggs to chicks to adult birds.

I watched him build the nesting-box
with large sure hands, drive nails true,
cut and sand the entrance to smooth.

I've watched him fix it above the tank,
watched the starlings reconnoitre,
enter and re-enter with strings of grass.

Now there are eggs; four eggs; pale blue
freckled brown. He and I are counting days.
10, 11, 12 – soon there will be nestlings.

Christ! What is he doing, the man? Why
does he enter his hand in the entrance hole
in the starling's absence, palm and heft her eggs?

My mind flaps with questions. Someone else
tells me, for the man sidesteps my eyes.
He is fingertapping for imminent fracture –

when the triangular gap breaches the shell

when slimed baldiness of fledgling dints
his finger, he'll feed them to his falcons.

Separating Eggs

Nan's practised fingers preparing meringue
– quick one-two-three flick of her hand –
two perfect shell-halves arced into the bin.

Do I remember, or was it a story, one about
a bad girl who threw shells on the fire,
stupid girl who stopped all the hens laying?

Ma's stainless steel fingers slicing toast soldiers
guillotining the head off the egg with a buttery knife.
A bad girl with a mouth compressed to a line –

a naughty bad child who'll never grow big with furious
tears at the soliders' forced entry, yolk on her chin.
Or is it a story?

There are hags in my kitchen – crowds of them
with similar features. They're laughing over some task
in common – weaving or cooking – I can't make it out.

Their disembodied voices are snarling my fingers up,
clumsying the tips so I can't get the cut clean enough,
the crack sharp enough, the timing spot-on.

Till I get it right, my soufflés will never rise.

Gifts

I am no lover of chocolate.
Savour and spice mean more to me
than sweet. They know it.

For Easter they have given me
a Chinese painted egg, ten open
anemones and a homemade card.

I assault the grain of their cheeks
with great smacking kisses till they smile
their pinkest smiles. I smile too,

savouring the notion of cuckoos
offering gifts of egg to repay
and say thank you.

Oh, it's cupboard love (they know somewhere
I have chocolate eggs for them) but
as cupboard lovers they are truly authentic,

big grabbing greedy beautiful chicks.
Look at their light blue eyes, pale skin,
straight fall of hair –

it's passing strange how they resemble me,
except they're chocolate-lovers.

Lemon Soufflé Omelette

This is a light, foamy, lemony pudding, literally made in moments
(Delia Smith's Cookery Course, Part 1)

There are just the two of them.

The woman has separated her eggs.
Now she is adding bitter and sharp,
now sweet. Now she is whisking them.
Now she is cooking them, folding
and stirring to prevent them sticking.

Look at her face as she carried the dish to the table,
the lighted brandy playing its blues on the surface
of what she's produced. Is it appetite, or pride
or simple pleasure that turns her mouth up so in its U?
Or is it that it took so few moments to make
and will serve two people?

Thinking Egg

In the warm kitchen
two women are sitting
confiding failings, fears.
One woman is me.

. . . like an egg I'm saying
one minute tough enough
to withstand anything, next
a fingertip could crack me. . .

The other woman is literal –
she'll have no truck with metaphor
No she's saying *No you are not*
an egg   You are a woman

and yes, my literal friend,
I guess you are right,
but I'm a woman thinking egg
and staggering under its weight.

DON PATERSON

A Private Bottling (1993)

Back in the front room that, an hour before
we led, lamp by lamp, into the darkness,
I sit down, turn the radio on low
as the last girl on the planet still awake
reads a dedication to the ships
and puts on a recording of the ocean.
I have evenly spaced out a chain of nips
in a big fairy-ring, in every glass
the tincture of a failed geography,
its dwindling burns and forests, whin-fires, heather,
the sklent of its wind and its salty rain,
the love-worn habits of its working folk,
their speech, and by imaginative extension
how they sing, make love or tell a joke.
So I have a good nose for this sort of thing.
I will take each fierce kiss smack on the lips
and let their gold tongues slide along my tongue
as each gives up, in turn, its little song
of the patient years in glass and sherryoak,
its shy negotiations with the sea,
the soil, the trick of how the peat-smoke
was locked inside it like a black thought.

Tonight I toast her with the extinct malts
of Ardlussa, Ladyburn and Dalintober
and an ancient pledge of passionate indifference,
ochón ó do dhóigh mé mo chlairseach ar a shon,
over and over and over, till I believe it.
When the circle is closed and I have drunk myself sober
I will tilt the blinds a little, and watch

the dawn grow in a glass of liver salts,
wait for the birds, the milk float's sweet nothings,
then slip back to the bed where she lies curled,
replace her warm ass in my freezing lap
gently, like a live egg in the wrong nest,
as dead to her as she is to the world.

Here we are again; it is precisely
twelve, fifteen or thirty years later,
exactly one turn up the spiral chamber
that is the sum of what I can remember.
Each glass holds its micro-episode
in suspension, till it plays again,
revivified by a suave connoisseurship
that deepens in the silence and the dark
to something like an infinite sensitivity.
This is not romantic conceit; get this – my father
used to know a man who'd taste the sea,
then leave his nets strung out along the bay
because there were no fish in it that day.
Everything is in everything else. It is a matter
of attunement, as once, through the hiss and backwash
I steered the dial into the voice of God
slightly to the left of Hilversum,
almost drowned by some big, blurry waltz
the way Sirius obscured its dwarf companion
for centuries, till someone thought to look.
In this way, I can isolate the feints
of feminine effluvia, carrion, shit,
those rogues and toxins only introduced
to give the composition a little weight
as rough harmonics do the violin-note
or Pluto, Chiron and the lesser saints
might do to our lives, for all you know.
(By God, you would recognise their absence

as anyone would testify, having sank
a glass of *North British*, run off a patent still
in some godforsaken satellite of Edinburgh;
a bleak spirit, no amount of caramel
could sweeten or disguise, its after-effect
somewhere between a blanket bath and a sad wank.
There is, no doubt, a bar in Lothian
where it is sworn upon and swallowed neat
by furloughed riggers and the Special Police,
men who hate the company of women).

Oh whiskies of Long Island and Provence!
This little number catches at the throat
but is all sweetness in the finish, my palate
counting through burning brake-fluid, nicotine,
pastis, Diorissimo and wet grass.
Here is another, all smiles and lip-service
with a kick like a smacked face in a train station.
Frost, semen, hashish, oblivion. I could go on forever.
A toast, then, since tonight I take the waters
with the more than simply absent: all the friends
we did not make, our faceless ushers, bridesmaids,
our four Shelties, three now ghosts of ghosts;
so here's tae us, wha's like us, damn few
and they're a' deid, or even less than deid,
our douce sons and our lovely loud-mouthed daughters
who will, at this late hour, be fully grown,
perhaps with unborn children of their own.
Don't be fooled; this is never true
feeling, but is sentimental residue.
This time, I will get away Scot-free
and die before her absence touches me.

PAUL FARLEY

Laws of Gravity (1995)

I found a guidebook to the port he knew
intimately – its guano coated ledges,
its weather-vanes, his bird's-eye view
of liner funnels, coal sloops and dredgers.
It helped me gain a foothold – how he felt
a hundred rungs above a fifties street,
and whether, being so high, he ever dwelt
on suicide, or flummoxed his feet
to last night's dancesteps, still fresh in his head.
It's all here in his ledger's marginalia:
how he fell up the dark stairwell to bed
and projected through to Australia;
and said a prayer for rainfall every night
so he could skip his first hungovered round.
The dates he's noted *chamois frozen tight
into bucket.* When he left the ground
a sense of purpose overtook and let
a different set of laws come into play:
like muezzins who ascend a minaret
to call the faithful of a town to pray.
Take one step at a time. Never look down.
He'd seen the hardest cases freeze halfway,
the arse-flap of their overalls turn brown.
As a rule, he writes, *your sense of angle
becomes acute at height.* A diagram
he's thumbnailed shows a drop through a triangle
if you miscalculated by a gramme.
Sometimes, his sense still blunted from booze,
he'd drop his squeegee, watch it fall to earth
and cling onto the grim hypotenuse

of his own making for all he was worth.
He seems to have enjoyed working that hour
The low sun caught the glass and raised the ante
On every aerial, flue and cooling tower,
And gilded the lofts, the rooftop shanty
Town, when everything was full of itself
And for a while even the Latin plaques
Ignited with a glow of squandered wealth.
At times like these I see what our world lacks,
The light of heaven on what we've produced
and here some words lost where his biro bled
then *clouds of dark birds zero in to roost.*
There's IOUs and debtors marked in red
and some description of the things he saw
beyond the pane – a hard-lit typing pool,
a room of faces on some vanished floor
closed-off and absolute like some fixed rule.
His story of the boy butting a wall,
the secretary crying at her desk,
all happened in the air above a mail.
Each edifice, each gargoyle and grotesque
is gone. The earliest thing I remember:
as our van dropped a gear up Brownlow Hill
I looked back at the panes of distemper
that sealed a world. We reached our overspill,
and this is where our stories overlap.
The coming of the cradle and sheet glass
was squeezing out the ladder and the slap
of leather into suds, and less and less
work came through the door. And anyway
you were getting tool old for scaling heights.
Now, when I change a bulb or queue to pay
at fairs, or when I'm checking-in for flights,
I feel our difference bit down to the quick.
There are no guidebooks to that town you knew

and this attempt to build it, brick by brick,
descends the page. I'll hold the foot for you.

B A HUMAR

Technical Assistance (1998)

The President is sitting in the garden of the palace
surrounded by his extended family – wife,
cousins, nieces, several uncles
by marriage, and a personal bodyguard
in American fatigues carrying
Kalashnikov automatic rifles.

The lawns are green and well cut
with bougainvillaea along the borders.
In the centre of the lawn is a large tree,
a Cedar of Lebanon, which provides shade
and respite from the sun. It is famously known,
and featured on stamps, as "The President's Tree".

Apart from the soldiers and servants, I
am the only man in the palace garden
without a tie. It is five o'clock
in the afternoon and still very hot.
I am waiting to be asked to present myself
officially to the President under the tree.

Two hours ago it seemed perfectly
reasonable to wear my light grey
tropical suit, open at the neck,
spotless, almost new and certainly
well-pressed. That was,
as it turned out, an error of judgement.

Although not desperately serious
(no socks would have been suicidal),

my offence is an affront to the President
and to the occasion, and cannot there
go unpunished. 'Tieless in Gaza',
I mutter, sweating under the hot sun.

The visitors – all except me,
that is – have now been presented
to the President, and are standing around chatting
in the shade of the President's Tree.
I can hear the President explaining: *'Psalms. . .
104, you know. . . Cedar of Libanus.'*

I have met the President several times
already. He knows me as the newly appointed
Advisor for Fine Arts and Museums –
'on loan from London' is his way
of putting it; but I have not yet been
formally presented at a President's reception.

Tea is being served in the deep
cool shade of the tree (milk
or lemon, Madam?), there are thinly-cut
cucumber sandwiches. And suddenly
I am noticed, ushered in from the heat
to the presence of His Excellency.

He smiles apologies – he hadn't realised
I was there as a guest. *'You are so familiar –
like an Old Master, already known
before encountered.'* I am the ancien
régime discredited. *'Please mention
my Degas to the French Ambassador,'* he says.

The guests assume I am one of the household,
an intimate in casual dress, just in
from the hills, perhaps. The family, extended
under the Cedar tree, believes
I am an esoteric freak. In London
I am registered as Technical Assistance.

I mingle with the guests, but clearly
am not accepted as one of them (no tie
must, after all, mean something).
'This tree' I am asked by a couple –
handsome, pleasantly seductive – *'surely it was here long
before Independence?'*

They are English, holding on to a memory
of Empire and fair play. The invitation
is clear: recognition, complicity, guile,
and a sporting option on betrayal.
Let's just, their faces smile, at least
agree on history and the true facts.

I am, I suppose, a guardian of history
and the true facts: *'Ah yes'*, I reply,
*'but you see, the President has given trees status –
it's our new conservation policy'* –
the best I can do, tieless in Africa,
at the end of a long century.

HENRY SHUKMAN

Ararat (2000)

It wus never a flud, they got it all rong.
It wus a heetwave. Who ever herd of a flud
In the desert? As if we wud hav minded!
We didn't pich up on that peek to keep dry
but cool. You cant imagine the heet.
It rold in like invisibal fire, like lions breth.
Never mind an eg you cud fry a stake
on a rock, and in the shade. Sandals smoked
with evry step. You had to wear 2 pairs
and even then run. Sleeping – a nitemare,
a joke. The only way to lie down wus to souse
yor bed evry our with water – warm water –
if you cud find it. Who wonts to shlep
to the well and back 6 times a nite?
For shlep I meen skip. Forget dreems.
Dreems evaporated befor they cud reech us.

We took to a cave. It wus cool as buchers
at ferst. Cudnt beleev our luck, problem solvd,
wed wait it out. We hung blankits over the mouth
to keep out the heet. Then dusnt the erth
heet up round us like an uven. The place ternd
into a bakers. The animals started showing up,
limping, wining. The lions came ferst and purd
at the blankits. I let them in. The lady nuzzeld
my elbow, lickt my hand with that scraper-
tongue of hers. She drew blud but didn't meen to
and never came back for mor. They straggled
past our pots and rugs, curld up in the caves dark.
After that we cud hardly refuse the rest.

In they cum, 2 by 2 trew enough.
Grunts, grumbles, grones. Mones and mews,
wines and wimpers. Clucks, chirrups,
werrings, buzzes, wissals, flooting.
Piping, worbling, fluttering, droning.
Berps, farts, sies, you name it we herd it.
The cave fild with the gurgels of a milion
animal slumbers. Youd think it wudve stunk
but the mingeld odors of a milion beests
wer sweet to the nostril like a bloom of flours.
And the dung? Strange but there was nun.

The sky ternd yellow. We stopt eeting.
The apitite dusnt do well at that heet.
We neither slept nor woke. Ime no hero
but sumthing had to be dun. So I organize
the boys. We lit a fire outside, wated til
the coles glowed then herded the lot strate out
onto them. The trick is once theyve been over
those coles the ground dusnt seem so hot.
A quick shock and you can handel anything.
Shem led the way: up the hill to the top.

We capt the peek up there like a nippal.
It wusnt exactly cool but we had a chance.
The sky wus blew agen for 1 thing.
Down below all you cud see wus yellow fog.
No ground, no hills. We hung on our iland of air.
So cleer up there, cleer as a shaving mirrer.
You hav a good long look at yourself
at a time like that. I didn't like wot I saw:
greed and mor greed. Iternal dissatisfaction.
Therst does funny things to you.
I even wept. I had no teers of corse

but I felt the rivulets of dust on my cheek
like guttermarks on brick. I felt rite to weep.

Its trew a duv flew up to us. A speck
shivring in the haze below, it flapt itself
into shape like a mirage cuming up
from the fog. It lit on my sholder,
put its beek to my eer to whisper sumthing –
the sweetest message ever herd.
Tho I cudnt make it out at ferst,
not until I put my finger in my eer.
I drew it out cool, damp: a drop of water
bellying on the end of it. I tried to shout
the news but my throte wudnt make a sound.

The ferst drops steemd, sizzeld and stung.
By then I didnt no if any 1 in the sprall
of flesh wus alive still. But as the rain fell
I herd mones and yelps all round, a crazy
dog barkt up at the thunderheds
in a rage, a fox howled, the frogs flooted
like an organ. Necks rose like plant stems.
Wite clouds bloomd up from the yellow fog.
I cried wen I saw them. I new we had wun.
Thats the trooth. I never got my voice back
so I cudnt put rite the talk of fluds.
Not until I lernt pen and ink. And I wus
eity when it happened not 8 hundred.
If I liv to 2 hundred IIe be happy. A drop
just fell on my page. I luv the rain, who dusnt.
Anuther drop. Like littal berries, spattrings
of juce were they hit my ink. I let them be.
Be the teers I cudnt cry. The Lords dew.

MARIO PETRUCCI

Half Life (2002)

*'If the scientists know nothing, if the writers
know nothing, then it's for us to help them
with our lives and our death.'*

> Svetlana Alexievich
> 'Voices from Chernobyl'

Do not kiss him they said, starting back, as though
he were an animal in its cot cocking its head to listen

but understanding nothing. *Do you understand? Are you
pregnant? No? And find him milk. Three litres a day.*

I poured that whiteness into him. Felt I was feeding
a goose its own feathers. He retched and cursed –

the thin dribble each side of his mouth worse than a child.
Each time you hold his hand is a year off your life. Can you

*hear us? His bones are more active than the Core.
Understand? That is no longer your husband.* I boiled

chickens until the bones sagged, fresh, handfuls of parsley
chopped so fine it melted between finger and thumb,

pot barley, apples (from Michurinsk they told me) pared
and pulped, everything minced and sieved, every trace

of rind or pip removed, no husk or shell or pod, and all of it
spewed back down his chest as though he could not take

a single particle more. The skin of his forearms and thighs
cracked like black pastry. His eyelids puffed and swelled

to blind him with blood. The lightest sheet peeled away
fat as flypaper, the slightest edge of thumbnail was to him

more vicious than any cut-throat – if I moved his head
he left hairs on the pillow as though he were a used match,

if I pushed a thumb into him – our wedding flesh – the indent
remained like hot grey putty, he coughed bile, acid, froth

and lunch, shreds of stomach lining and liver and still he
stayed – refused that first, that last, step onto his Jacob's Ladder.

Those reptile eggs of his eyelids, turned always towards me.
Until I said Go, I love you. But Go. Until that moment

I still believed I would save him. Milk, soup, kisses. As if
he could digest the touch of my lips, feel my making of broth

in his dissolving heart-chambers. When his breath shut,
when he began to cool – then, I called for family. It was

almost a miracle, the Doctors said. Forty times the fatal dose
and he nearly turned round. I felt myself the wrong side

of a door – a partition thin as plywood, thinner, as though
you could hear everything that was going on inside.

His mother hugged me. The brothers kissed me. Now we
are your brothers. Have you ever been the wrong side

of that door, knowing all you needed was the key and you
could walk straight in? That's how it was. We were that close.

They had to teach me
from scratch. Teach me

to breathe. As though
I had fallen out of space or

up from water and breath
was labour – each breath

a pang to draw me back
from the brink. In. Out. In

this world life is indifferent.
You must will it in. Will it

out. I look at my son –
those white cheeks that

pinched brow and
I wonder how I can

breathe. He says – *Mama*
when you go to sleep to-

night please don't forget to
breath. Please. He is

not allowed to run. Or
jump. Like that boy who

hanged himself with a
belt. I watch him. And he

watches me – when I doze on
the red sofa he places a

hand to check the rise and
fall of my chest. Tells me he

will teach me in his dreams –
will teach me to breath if

I teach him how to fly. *If
you go with Grandpa he*

*says, will you be able to
breathe?* – he says this and

his cheeks run wet and
he runs short of breath so

we sit and teach each
other once again how to –

deep and slow. *We are
flying,* I tell him. *We are*

breathing, he replies.
'My parents kissed – and I was born'

Then black clouds. Black rain.
Our garden all white. Not a white
like snow – but glass. Grandma
told me to count my sins. We were
down in the cellar. I expected the devil
to burst through the bricks with all
his heat behind him. I saw the frog
me and Vadik burst with a stick. How
its insides came out red like the jam
I dropped that made mama swear.

Dad came home black. Not his
clothes. His face. He said he got
too close. We visited him in a white
room. A man chased Kitty with a Geiger
– he tried to put the clicks on Kitty's tail
like salt. He had a big plastic bag. Got
angry when I giggled, when I shouted
Run Kitty! Then Dad got angry too.

Some old women met the train
when we stopped. They threw
brown stones at us. Then we saw
it was bread. I asked one for water.
She looked like Grandma. She made
the sign of the cross. Took one step
back. A woman in a white apron
brought us ice-cream. She let us
keep the glass. Then soldiers came –
kept washing our train. I looked for
the old woman, the one who looked
like Grandma. But she was gone.

A man in a white spacesuit and mask
met us at the hospital. He said – *Put
all your clothes in this bag.* I thought
about Kitty. I didn't laugh. He said
he was a doctor but I didn't believe him.
He didn't look like the doctors you see
in the films. I was crying but happy

I would see the city. From the window
the city was grey. Now if a bee stings,
you die. At night I look out the window
to see if there is a fox with three tails.
I will go to sleep. I will go to sleep

forever. And become science.

I dreamed I was dead – but
mama was crying in the dream.
She cried so loud it woke me up.
She woke me up so I wouldn't die.
But when I looked around for her
she wasn't there. They take me to her
on Tuesday. *Remember, she can't
talk.* That's what he says – the man
who thinks he is a doctor. But he's
wrong. Mama talks to me. She
talks with her eyes. Mama told me –
We all come back as someone else.
Vadik told me my parents kissed
and I was born. I will find a boy
in the ward. A boy like Vadik.
And kiss him.

They put me in a white room.
To paint. No one hugs me.
Under the window is a nest.
I wait to see if there are babies.
To see if the daises will open –
if they are black. A woman with
red hair looks at what I paint.
She sits with her hands folded.
Says her name is not important.
I make a painting and she holds it
up to the window. Like X-rays.
She says – *Are all your people
black?* I don't answer. I twist
my brush in the paint. The way
Dad would do with his fork
in spaghetti. I pick up as much

of the dark as I can. I ask him
for more – the man who pretends
to be a doctor. I tell him. *There
is never enough black.*

*nana? what is
radiation?* Ah – it is

everywhere little one.
All around us.

*but nana   can you
see it?*

No.
can you smell it?

No.
can you touch it? is it

hot? No
my little Matryushka.

*but i can taste it   i think
i can   can you*

taste it nana?
Perhaps. But I am

buried deep.
nana   i think i heard it

*in a dream
in a little voice in my ear*

all crackly
and silly   like our radio

that never works
And what did it say?

i don't know   i couldn't
hear

Never mind. Sleep now –
go to sleep. I am tired.

nana   can we count the numbers
together?

Alright. Are you ready?
anna   eva   vasily

alexandr   mikhail   sofia
borisovna   nikolai

– nana   did i remember
them all?

Yes. Now close your eyes.
It is time to sleep.

nana   tell me
is radiation

like god?

*

This hospital has a room
for weeping. It has no crèche,

no canteen. No washroom queue.
Only this queue for weeping.

No lost property booth. No
complaints department. No

reception. No office of second
opinion, of second chances. Its sons

and daughters die with surprise
in their faces. But mothers

must not cry before them. There is
a room for weeping. How hard

the staff are trying. Sometimes
they use the rooms themselves. They

must hose it out each evening.
The State is watching. They made

this room for weeping. No remission.
No quick fixes. A father wonders

if his boy is sleeping. A mother
rakes her soul for healing. Neighbours

in the corridor – one is screaming
It moved from your child to mine.

More come in. Until the lino
blurs with tears and the walls

are heaving. Until the place can't
catch its breath – stale breath

of pine. And at its heart
this room.

*

In a dream he has
no shoes. He tells me
Buy slippers. The largest

you can find. Put them
on the lid of a coffin
with my name inside.

Write it on a slip of paper
and put it inside – I will
find them. We are all

in the same place here.
I remember the grey stumps.
Their five clouded lenses

of toenail. E*lephant*
he said. I am an elephant.
Forget nothing. You must not

forget. Give me back
my flesh. They stole it
from me. Find my flesh.

Once he said – *Man shoots*
but God carries the bullets.
What now? How grey

Here, he says, *cats eat*
tomatoes. They eat kittens
to purge themselves.

The dog waits at the gate
for his master – nothing
but ear and bone. Did they

lay me on the door
of our house, my brothers?
Did I die? And now

our daughter. Her hairless
body. Oh love. I am all bone
here. Bring me slippers.

*

Take our words. Enrich them.
They are already active, but enrich them.

This is dangerous. May even be impossible.
They are dispersed through a great mass

and you may need to convert this vast mass
to elicit one small grain. You may have

to detach yourself. Use robots and machines.
But at the end – after immense effort – you

will make of our cries a single silver rod.
You will put it on display behind a screen.

Your scientists will marvel. Your politicians
quake. You will have to control and subdue it –

contain it with great care. Many will not wish
to have it near them, or their children. You will

protect yourself with suits. Put your ear to it
and hear it hum. It will make you shudder.

One night – in early darkness. When you are
thinking of something else. It will escape.

JOE KANE

The Boy Who Nearly Won The Texaco Art Competition (2004)

he took a large sheet
of white paper and on this
he made the world an african world
of flat topped trees and dried grasses
and he painted an elephant in the middle
and a lion with a big mane and several giraffes
stood over the elephant and some small animals to fill
in the gaps he worked all day had a bath this was saturday

on sunday he put six jackals
in the world and a great big snake
and buzzards in the sky and tickbirds
on the elephants back he drew down blue
from the sky to make a river and got the elephants
legs all wet and smudged and one of the jackals got drowned
he put red flowers in the front of the picture and daffodils in the bottom corners
and his dog major chewing a bone and mrs murphys two cats tom and jerry
and milo the milkman with a cigarette in the corner of his mouth
and his merville dairy float pulled by his wonder horse trigger
that would walk when he said click click and the holy family
in the top right corner with the donkey and cow
and sheep and baby jesus and got the 40A bus
on monday morning in to abbey street to hand
it in and the man on the door said
thats a sure winner

ARVON

The Foundation for Writing

The Arvon Foundation is the leading national charity devoted to the open access encouragement and teaching of creative writing at every level through week long residencies, led by published writers.

Through a combination of its open courses for adults, its tailor-made schools courses, and unique partnerships with groups such as the Medical Foundation for the Care of Victims of Torture and Graeae Theatre – all held at one of the four regional residential centres throughout the UK – Arvon promotes the power of self expression and development through the written word, encouraging and enabling young people, adults and writers-to-be to explore their creative potential in a supportive environment.

In this way, Arvon has contributed, since its founding in 1968, to the creative life of the UK, as well as the promotion and development of literature. Writers such as Simon Armitage, Pat Barker, Tunita Gupta, Lemm Sissay and Esther Freud are just a few of the many writers who have all started their writing lives on Arvon courses. The list reads like a roll call of the British literary scene past, present and future.

Arvon's commitment to open access is reflected in the fact that no qualifications are needed to go on any of its course, and there is a bursary scheme to help people on low incomes. Arvon provides uniquely the space, time and place, away from everyday life, for people from diverse backgrounds, ages and abilities to concentrate on exploring and extending their creative potential through the power of writing. People attending just need to provide the willingness and ability to learn and enjoy in some of the most beautiful countryside Britain has to offer.

ABOUT THE ARVON INTERNATIONAL POETRY COMPETITION

This is the thirteenth Arvon International Poetry Competition organised by the Arvon Foundation. The competition is held every other year and we are delighted at the response it receives. Each and every poem is judged anonymously and this helps to attract established poets as well as those yet to be published. We at Arvon have been thrilled by the standard of this year's entries and have gained immense pleasure from reading the winning and commended poems chosen by the judges. With the past winning poems as well – from every competition back to the first in 1980 – we hope you enjoy this bumper collection of poems, each a winner, each different in so many ways.

This book and the competition have helped us to raise much needed funds. The money will provide grants, help us to maintain our writing centres and subsidise the cost of Arvon writing courses. We are grateful to all the poets who entered the poems, to our judges, and to Farrer & Co., The Times and Classic FM for their help in publicising the competition.

We look forward to the next competition in 2008, when Arvon celebrates its fortieth anniversary as a leading provider of creative writing courses in the UK.

Best wishes
Ariane Koek
Director

Further information is available from

The Arvon Foundation
42a Buckingham Palace Road
London
SW1W 0RE

T 020 7931 7611
E london@arvonfoundation.org
W www.arvonfoundation.org